DATE DUE

FEB 0 3 2011	
FEB 2 2 2011	
OCT 0 9 2014	

BRODART, CO.   Cat. No. 23-221

When Mothers Kill

Michelle Oberman and Cheryl L. Meyer

When Mothers Kill

Interviews from Prison

New York University Press • *New York and London*

NEW YORK UNIVERSITY PRESS
New York and London
www.nyupress.org

Library of Congress Cataloging-in-Publication Data
Oberman, Michelle.
When mothers kill : interviews from prison / Michelle Oberman and
Cheryl L. Meyer.
p.   cm.
Includes bibliographical references and index.
ISBN-13: 978-0-8147-5702-4 (cl : alk. paper)
ISBN-10: 0-8147-5702-2 (cl : alk. paper)
1. Women prisoners—United States—Interviews. 2. Women murderers—
United States—Interviews. 3. Filicide—United States—Case studies.
4. Infanticide—United States—Case studies. 5. Ohio Reformatory for Women.
I. Meyer, Cheryl L., 1959– II. Title.
HV9471.O34 2008
364.152'308520973—dc21   2007049410

New York University Press books are printed on acid-free paper,
and their binding materials are chosen for strength and durability.

Manufactured in the United States of America

c 10 9 8 7 6 5 4 3 2 1
p 10 9 8 7 6 5 4 3 2 1

In gratitude to all whose love weaves my safety net: my partner and my children, big and little; my mother; my friends; and the memory of my father, who loved me very much. — MO

To Deb, Rachel, and Sara. You are the best. — CM

Contents

Acknowledgments

We will be forever indebted to the women we interviewed for pouring their hearts out to us and sharing their stories.

We cannot begin to express our gratitude to Dr. Karen Dapper and the staff of mental health services at the Ohio Reformatory for Women (ORW). Thank you for your hospitality and cooperation. It is evident that you not only care for the women but care about the women.

Cindy Weisbart provided the impetus for these interviews by undertaking them as part of her dissertation. Cindy worked on the structure and design of the initial set of interviews and co-facilitated and transcribed the first twelve. Thank you, Cindy, for your inspiration and your tenacity.

The remaining interviews were co-facilitated and transcribed by Michelle Rone, Kelly White, Dawn Bramley, Abby Goldstein, and Thelia Jackson. We are grateful to you for all your work and for driving to rural Ohio in the dark on frosty mornings. We appreciate your persistence despite impediments and disruptions.

We would also like to thank our editor, Jennifer Hammer, who has been with us through numerous crises and not made us feel too bad about missing deadlines.

Katherine K. Baker, Sarah K. Delson, Larry Marshall, and Karen Dapper all provided invaluable editorial assistance. Although all errors are our own, we know that this final draft is better for your wise counsel.

Michelle would also like to thank Printer's Café in Palo Alto, California, which, for the small price of a morning latte, became for her a writer's studio and a phone-conference center while we worked on this book.

Research assistance for this book was provided by Mary Colleen Ryan (Santa Clara University School of Law, class of 2008).

We are grateful to our respective institutions, Santa Clara University School of Law and Wright State University School of Professional Psychology, both of which generously supported our research by providing us with time and resources.

Finally, we are grateful to our families for us allowing us to take the time we needed to focus on this project and for tolerating the occasional mental and emotional distance it created. This project made us appreciate all of you so much more.

Introduction

WHY WOULD ONE even want to talk to a mother who killed her children? So horrific is this crime that the thought of sitting in the same room with such a person brings a twinge of revulsion, an involuntary shiver, even after having spent hours in conversation with these very women. But now, at least for us, the revulsion is directed outward, at the crime, rather than at the women themselves.

We set out to speak with mothers who kill because, after almost two decades of studying these women's cases, we realized that no one had ever really talked to them.[1] Many had told their stories for them — experts, journalists, lawyers — but no one had ever asked the women if these stories had gotten it right, or even whether they had some thoughts of their own on what had gone wrong.

We turned to the mothers themselves, asking them to tell us their stories — not just the stories of how they killed their children but also the stories that might help us to understand why, and maybe how, it might have been prevented. We asked them to tell us their stories about who they were, before and after their crimes, stories of how they had lived, what they had expected from life and from themselves. We asked about their lives as children, as young women, and as mothers; about love and stress; and about their coping mechanisms and support systems. We asked about their experiences with the various agencies designed to support and protect vulnerable citizens and about their interactions with the criminal justice system.

We asked them these questions not because we expected that their answers somehow would be more "true" than those ascertained through the legal or health care systems. We fully expected them to tell versions of their stories that were defensive and self-serving. We asked them because we sought their unique perspective and insight into the events — their own explanations of what happened and why.

These women can tell us about their lives as they were living them in the years, weeks, and days before they killed their children. They offer us a meaningful understanding of the factors that contributed to their children's deaths and of the things that might have prevented them. Their stories shine a light on the path to preventing filicide, the killing of a child by a parent. They are as enlightening as they are terrifying.

Our conversations with mothers who killed their children left us feeling humbled and less sure of our capacity to assess others. We spent many long days listening to their stories in an eight-by-ten cinderblock room with a single window too high for a view, covered with bars. Their stories placed the abundance in our lives into stark relief, causing us to see the intricately woven fabric that sustains us. All the people who have cared for us, the places in which we feel safe, the beauty in even the worst days suddenly became visible. This fabric lifts and carries us through our lives. It was there all along, but we did not know it.

Prior Research

Our original work on mothers who kill their children, including our previous book, *Mothers Who Kill Their Children*,[2] was devoted, in large part, to describing the patterned nature of the crime of maternal filicide. We surveyed hundreds of newspaper stories, and available medical and social science articles, to identify a set of five markedly distinct categories of mothers who kill. The newspaper articles afforded us an emotional distance from this tragic subject matter. We could keep the nightmare at bay, taking in the familiar patterns in each new story without having to sense the grief that each lost life demands of us. We focused on the ways that cases were similar to one another, and then on the ways in which they were different. We identified five categories of maternal filicide: neonaticide, or filicide related to an ignored pregnancy; abuse-related filicide; filicide due to neglect; assisted/coerced filicide; and purposeful filicide, in which the mother acted alone.

Years of working on this subject made us aware of the missing pieces when we discussed these cases. To think about why a mother would do so heinous a thing to her child, one has to make an intuitive leap, trusting that one knows enough about her life to understand her actions. But the truth is that we do not know nearly enough about these women's lives to make such assumptions.

The fundamental contribution of this volume is to begin filling in the missing pieces of these stories by creating a record of the conversations that we held with forty women who were incarcerated for killing their children. Our conversations with the women began in 2001, when we spoke, in two- to three-hour-long sessions, with women serving time for homicide at the Ohio Reformatory for Women (ORW). The methods by which we identified these women, and the questionnaire that formed the template for these conversations, are discussed in appendix A, at the conclusion of this book.

After we finished our interviews, we were struck by certain themes and patterns. We wanted to be sure that we had heard them correctly. Rather than reinterview everyone with whom we had spoken, we decided to speak once again, at greater length, with a subset of eight of these women. In considering which women to reinterview, we were limited by the fact that many of our original participants had completed their sentences and were no longer incarcerated. We attempted to select a representative sample, while also looking to speak with those who had been particularly forthcoming.

In 2006 we reinterviewed these eight women,[3] asking them to expand more fully on the themes they had raised in our initial conversations and inviting them to reflect on how they viewed themselves and their crimes from this juncture. The questionnaire used to guide these conversations appears in appendix A. Because we rely so heavily on the stories told by these eight women, we have summarized each of their lives into "narratives," which are presented in chapter 1, and are prominently featured in the chapters that follow.

Our interviews with women incarcerated for the crime of homicide confirmed our earlier research. Our conversations with women who committed neonaticide supported our first book's findings regarding the emotional isolation and terror experienced by those who conceal or deny their pregnancies and then kill the infant within twenty-four hours of birth. Our discussions with women whose children were killed in neglect-related incidents revealed, as expected, young single mothers of multiple children, whose lives were in a state of chaos at the time of their child's death.

Our research for this book could not, nor was it intended to, completely substantiate the findings of our first book. Although each of the various patterns of maternal filicide that we identified in our first book was represented by at least one of the women with whom we spoke, the number of stories representing any particular type of filicide was not necessarily proportional to its incidence. Approximately 70 percent of the women we interviewed represented three categories — abuse-related filicide, filicide due to neglect, and assisted/coerced filicide — although these particular types of filicide composed only 47 percent of the cases identified in our first book. The population of women we interviewed at ORW included relatively few women convicted of committing neonaticide and very few women who purposely killed their children.

The limited number of neonaticide stories told by the women with whom we spoke reflects the fact that neonaticide often is committed by girls who have not yet become legal adults. Many are punished as juvenile offenders; their records are sealed, their sentences are limited, and they are housed separately from the adult prisoners. Because neonaticide stories are so distinctly patterned, we have gathered the few stories we heard and retell them, amplified by existing scientific and social science literature, in appendix B.

The reasons underlying the relative paucity in our study of women who purposely killed their children stems from the nature of mental illness, as well as from the manner in which the criminal justice system responds to the mentally ill. There are a broad range of mental illnesses implicated in maternal filicide cases. Some mentally ill mothers who kill suffered from chronic, disabling conditions, such as schizophrenia, which were either undiagnosed or untreated at the time of their crimes. Others cases involve women who, at the time of their crimes, were experiencing a recurring condition, such as major depression, or an acute crisis, such as postpartum psychosis.[4]

In spite of the fact that there are many cases of filicide committed by women who are profoundly mentally ill, in Ohio and elsewhere, there were few such women incarcerated at the ORW at the time of our study. Prisoners with profound mental disorders may be housed in mental institutions rather than prisons. Some have never been tried for their crimes because they are not competent to stand trial. Others, particularly those suffering from an acute episode of mental illness, may have been adjudicated "not guilty for reason of insanity" and may not be incarcerated. Some deeply mentally ill women have been tried and convicted of homicide, but because their illnesses proved to be too hard to manage within the general prison population, they are housed separately, with other mentally ill prisoners. Finally, many mentally ill mothers who kill their children also kill themselves, at the same time that they kill their children or apart from that crime. Using available literature on mothers who kill and mental illness, appendix C attempts to tell the "missing story" of this group of filicidal mothers, often mothers who purposely killed their children.

The Stories and the Listeners: Emerging Themes

These stories can only tell us so much. There are limits inherent in the methodology. One limit on the implications of these stories lies in the distance between the storyteller and the listener. As listeners, our responses to the women's stories inevitably were bound up in our own realities and experiences. Although we shared a common vocabulary with the women whom we interviewed, our life experiences were so distinct as to render ambiguous even seemingly clear words, such as "home" or "good." We often had vastly different definitions of these words.

Several women described their childhoods as "happy" or "good" but told of homes that were rife with violence. When we asked one woman to tell us about her childhood, she began by saying, "Boy — well my life as a child was very happy. I was raised by my mom and stepfather." She went on to say:

> They were very strict. I was abused and beat, but never knew why. I was never a cheerleader or in groups, but I couldn't do anything — very sheltered. If I was late from school I was beaten, all the way through high school. Anything I did had to be during school. I have never been to a party to this day. . . . I ran away a couple of times.

As we undertook the task of retelling these women's stories, we struggled to highlight what the women considered important, the truth as they saw it, rather than simply recounting what struck us as noteworthy. A story takes on a new form as it is heard and retold, and undoubtedly, we have reconfigured these women's tales by virtue of what we deemed significant. This volume is as much a testament to our responses to their stories as it is an effort to tell them.

The core themes that emerged from our conversations involved violence, isolation, and hopelessness. Every woman with whom we spoke had been victimized by some form of violence. Violence was so common, and so endemic to their lives, that we found ourselves at first incredulous, and then simply weary. We longed to believe that they did not experience, or feel, the violence in the same way that we might have. Many were raped, and at such young ages, that we simply could not fathom what it would be like to try to live as an adult woman after having lived through that as a child. It was easier to hope that they did not experience rape as the same sort of horrific violation that it would be for us.

But their stories, as they told them, were not even about rape. Rape was mentioned only in passing. Nor were their stories necessarily about parental addiction, or child abuse, even though these things were present in almost all their stories. The effort to survive just one day of their childhoods would seem to entail soul-crushing grief. Yet, the women accepted their experiences as basic and normal, just as, in some ways, we all do our pasts. They offered up these stories about their lives not as explanations or as excuses, but as facts. This simply was how it was for them.

When love came, it came with a price tag. Your father, when you got to see him, beat you, or had sex with you, or both. Your mother gave you a place to live, but it was with her new husband and the children they had together, and none of them let you forget it, not even for a minute. Your boyfriend made you feel sexy, but he slept with other women, only saw you when he felt like it, teased you about being a dropout, beat you in front of your children, and sometimes beat your children. And there were no friends to rely on — no one to take your call, no one to help you determine what was normal, what was unacceptable, and how to chart a course to safety.

The lack of a safe haven amid the violence in their lives spoke to a deeper theme, one that linked virtually every story we heard — these women were profoundly isolated. Even among large, extended families, often there was no one paying attention to them, no one who cared deeply. The center of their lives seemed hollow.

Hope does not grow well in these environments. In order to have hope, one must believe in the possibility of change. It is hard to know whether children are born into hope or whether it must be cultivated. It is clear, though, that at some point in the months or even years leading to the horrific crimes these women committed, they lost faith in a future that looked any different. That despair lies at the core of their stories: there is the loss of even the hope for change.

There is a second limit in the methodology. By definition, these cases are nightmare scenarios. Many women are raised by unstable, abusive parents; many have intimate relationships marked by violence; many embark on motherhood at very young ages, isolated and lacking basic resources such as shelter and money, but they do not all kill their children. To date, there is no way to know how many other women survive precisely the same sort of circumstances described in these women's stories and do not kill their children.

Even though stories, rather than data points, form the foundation of this volume, the truths told are no less valid or legitimate. Like the parable of the blind men trying to describe the elephant,[5] each of the women's life stories, each of their versions of reality, is a partial truth. To the extent that we seek to make sense of the phenomenon of maternal filicide, these women's truths are vital to us.

Overview

This book proceeds in two parts. The first part of the book is devoted to retelling the women's stories and largely comprises their personal reflections on their lives and crimes. We begin our exploration of these mothers' journeys by highlighting the stories of eight women whom we were able to interview twice and whose stories reflect a broad cross section of the various types of filicide.[6] Their cases demonstrate the most common themes that emerged from the stories told by the mothers with whom we spoke.

The chapters that follow these case studies are devoted to an exploration of the various themes as they manifested in the women's lives. Chapter 2 recounts the stories that grew out of their own childhoods, focusing predominantly on their connections to their parents. Interestingly, the women spoke at far greater length about their connections to their mothers than they did to their fathers. This chapter is a testament to the ways in which their relationships with their mothers affected their own lives, both as children and as young mothers. In chapter 3 we consider their stories about romance, retracing both the women's descriptions of their relationships and the significance of romantic love in their lives. Chapter 4 turns to the subject of motherhood, in which the women discuss both their hopes and dreams as mothers and the distance between those dreams and the realities they encountered.

Part 1 of the book concludes with chapter 5, which examines the women's experiences in prison, telling their stories about their lives as incarcerated adults. In this chapter we hear the women's stories about shame and punishment, and also about reconciliation. These stories afford us the chance to consider these women's experiences within the criminal justice system: both the manner in which their particular case was adjudicated and the effect that incarceration has had on their lives.

Part 2 of the book sets a context, or backdrop, against which the women's stories, and the problem of maternal filicide in general, might better be understood. Chapter 6 discusses the social and institutional structures that framed these women's lives, as young children, as adolescents, as parents, and as adults. The women demonstrated an intimate familiarity with various state agents — social workers, welfare bureaucrats, housing officers, lawyers, probation officers, public health workers, school teachers, hospital personnel. These various government officials emerge as critical influences on the women's actions and choices. Chapter 6 also describes the manner in which the women worked to navigate their encounters with these various state agencies, attempting to avoid those that they perceived as potentially harmful, while accepting the involvement of others as inevitable or even desirable.

The book's final chapter reflects on the implications and questions raised by the stories these women have told us. In particular, we return to the question of whether women who commit filicide might be different, in meaningful ways, from others who seem to be similarly situated and do not harm their children. We explore the alternative policy implications for punishment and prevention that arise from our data.

At the end of the book, we take a step back from the individual components or themes in the women's stories and attempt to convey our sense of the whole — the confluence of factors that contributed to these mothers' crimes. We consider the nature of their profound isolation from support and the fact that it seems plausible, if not likely, that the presence of any one positive factor — a well-paying job, a loving spouse, a supportive family, a healthy coping mechanism for dealing with stress, an attentive case worker — might have saved these mothers and their children from their fate. Their depiction of the struggle to parent with too few resources offers a silent testimony to the fragile network that holds life together for the vast majority of mothers and children in this society. From them we learn a new story about what contributes to resilience and the ability to survive, and even to thrive, in times of great stress.

But all of this storytelling starts with the stories told by the women themselves, and it is to them that we now turn.

PART 1

The Stories

The following five chapters are organized around the central themes that emerged from our conversations with women incarcerated for killing their children. We have tried, insofar as possible, to represent their stories as they told them to us, inserting our personal perspectives only when it seemed important for reasons of clarity and honesty. The structure of these chapters, and the ideas around which they are framed, only emerged after our interviews with the women. Indeed, after we finished speaking with them, the themes underlying each chapter seemed almost obvious to us, and we felt as if there was no other way to tell these stories. This first part of our book, then, is devoted to a discussion of these themes. The second part undertakes the task of considering these stories as a whole, reflecting on their broader meaning and implications.

1

The Saddest Stories

THE CONVERSATIONS WE had with these women were emotional for all of us. The women often told us that this was the first time they had attempted to talk to anyone about the events surrounding their children's deaths. All the interviews took place at the Ohio Reformatory for Women (ORW). The women with whom we spoke represent a broad cross section of the U.S. population.

As is common in the U.S. prison population, women of color were overrepresented among the ORW population, when compared with their overall numbers in society. Indeed, of the forty women we interviewed, approximately 40 percent were women of color. For several reasons, we elected not to ask the women questions about their race, nor to focus on race in our analysis of our findings. In our sample, class, or socioeconomic status, was a far more salient factor in contributing to our understanding of this crime than factors such as race, ethnicity, or culture. In addition, a focus on race might have eclipsed the considerable diversity within the Caucasian population at the ORW, many of whom were from poor, rural Appalachian families.

Because the ORW is the only women's prison in Ohio, the women we met came from a wide range of communities, from rural Appalachia to large, inner-city housing projects. In addition, many of the women with whom we spoke lived significant portions of their lives, as children and as mothers, in other states. Their residence in Ohio at the time of their crimes was, in many cases, simply a coincidence.

In order to assist the reader, we have summarized in this first chapter the life stories told by these eight women. To insure anonymity, however, we have altered some of the details and have changed their names, and in some cases have paraphrased their actual words. We crafted the scenarios that follow by using information the women provided to us in both of their interviews. We chose not to add third-party information, such as official court records, but rather, to present their stories as they told them to us.

In addition to the eight stories told by these women, the chapters that follow include numerous comments and quotes drawn from the first set of interviews we conducted with the other thirty-two women. For simplicity's sake, we have not given these other women pseudonyms; we instead refer to them only as "one of the women with whom we spoke."

Nancy

Nancy's biological parents separated soon after her birth. Nancy's mother remarried and she had four half siblings. Nancy did not know until she was in her teens that her stepfather was not her biological father, although she had suspected it. As a child she was verbally and physical abused by her parents, and she was sexually molested until the age of ten by a male relative. When she told her mother about the abuse, her mother minimized and ignored her complaints.

Nancy did not get along well with her mother and stepfather. She frequently was blamed for any problems in the home. She described the environment in her home as unstable, with frequent fighting and arguing. Her mother often asked, or even forced her to leave home.

By the time she was in her teens, Nancy had many sexual partners. Her relationships were marked by domestic violence. Eventually, she became pregnant and had a child. Her relationship with her baby's father ended. She still lived with her mother and stepfather, although she fought with them constantly. For the next year and a half, she and her son moved from place to place. During this time, she became pregnant again.

After the birth of her second child, nineteen-year-old Nancy and her babies still did not have a stable home. During the first eight weeks after her second child was born, they lived in eleven different places, including a homeless shelter. Nancy thought that it was the time in the homeless shelter that was "the straw that broke the camel's back." She had no support, her baby was colicky, and Nancy felt that she did not know how to be a mother. On the day she smothered her child, Nancy said she just snapped. The baby was crying incessantly, and in an impulsive effort to quiet her, Nancy smothered her. She said that the baby's screaming reminded her of being screamed at by her parents, and she felt like she turned into her mother.

Nancy cries when she talks about her family and her surviving child. She said she talks to her son as a friend, because she feels that she does not have the right to be a mother. When we first interviewed Nancy, she worried about what she would tell him when he asked why she was incarcerated. Now, five years later, he knows. His approach to her is combative, and he has asked her, "What are you going to do, kill me too?"

Nancy says people have told her she could have more children when she is released, but she says she is not sure she is mentally stable enough to do so. She also feels that, even though she has completed parenting classes in prison, she still does not know how to be a mother. She says that she cries every day for her child and that it is especially hard during the holidays. Nancy said, "I think the hardest thing is forgiveness. I can forgive anyone else in a heartbeat. I am not a vicious person but I did this with my own hands."

Laurie

Laurie became pregnant during her freshman year of high school. By the time she was seventeen, she had two more children and had married their father. The relationship was abusive and ended suddenly when her husband died in an accident on Laurie's eighteenth birthday.

Soon after he died, Laurie learned she was pregnant again with his child. She felt she would be unable to handle another child, but she did not believe in abortion, so she decided to relinquish the child for adoption. Afterward, Laurie went on with her life, residing with her mother and stepfather, and enjoying her children. She recalls that they would walk to the park and go to the playground. One evening when her parents were out and while her children were asleep, a married friend of her parents dropped by for a visit and raped Laurie. Laurie never told anyone about this encounter because she was afraid, humiliated, and felt she should have fought back more.

Sometime later, Laurie realized that her rapist had impregnated her. Laurie concealed the pregnancy, and when she reflected on it during her first interview, she said, "That was the hardest part, ignoring my pregnancy. I had no medical care. I kept thinking 'This can't be true, this isn't happening to you.' Several times I tried to talk to my parents but I was too scared. I thought they would lose love for me or feel ashamed of me or think it was my fault." Laurie said she did not consider adoption because she would have had to reveal the pregnancy to her parents.

Laurie went into labor at home and delivered her baby in the bathroom. She doesn't remember what happened after she gave birth, but her newborn was dead. She was convicted and sentenced to fifteen years to life in prison.

She misses her children, who are being raised by her parents. Laurie sobbed during the entire interview on both occasions. Almost a decade after the death of her child, she remains emotionally raw. She frequently used the words "ashamed," "scared," "humiliated," and "guilty."

Nadine

Nadine was the older of two children, and her parents divorced when she was in fourth grade. Her mother went to live in another state with a new boyfriend, leaving her children behind with their abusive father. Nadine did not see her mother or know of her mother's whereabouts until she was nineteen. Nadine describes her father as frequently doing "disappearing acts." Whenever he reappeared, things would be okay for a short period, but then he would begin using alcohol and drugs and physically abusing her. When she entered puberty, he began sexually abusing her as well.

Eventually her father "dumped the kids" with their maternal grandparents. Nadine's grandmother was not well, so her grandfather was the main caretaker for the children. Over the next five years, Nadine moved frequently. She lived with her grandparents, her father, a foster family, and a couple for whom she worked as a nanny. She was pregnant by the time she was fourteen, but the pregnancy ended in a miscarriage. She gave birth to her first child when she was sixteen. The baby's father was the married man who had employed her as a nanny, who Nadine describes as having been a "kind man."

When she became pregnant, Nadine lost her job as a nanny and returned to her grandfather's home to have her baby. Within a year, she became pregnant with her second child and moved in with her boyfriend, Rusty. The relationship was marked by physical abuse and drug usage. Eventually the state Department of Children's Services removed the children from Nadine and Rusty's home because of neglect. In order to be reunited with her children Nadine had to follow a plan. She left Rusty, quit using drugs and alcohol, took parenting classes, and found a job. She was also seeking stable housing. That is when she met Mack.

Mack appeared to provide the stability Nadine needed in a relationship. Eventually they married, regained custody of Nadine's children, had two additional children of their own, and moved to Ohio to be closer to Mack's parents. After the move, Nadine began to notice erratic behavior from Mack. He became physically abusive toward her and verbally abusive toward the children. Nadine indicated that everyone in the small town in which they lived knew about the abuse but turned a deaf ear. She said that Mack's mother told her that if she "got an ass whipping, she deserved it." When Nadine found drug paraphernalia in their home, she decided to leave and began saving money to travel to another state.

One day Nadine's seven-year-old son, Josh, was cleaning the house when Mack began to berate him. Josh's paternal grandfather had told him that because Mack was not his father, he should just tell Mack that he did not have to listen to anything Mack had to say. When Josh said this, Mack erupted and beat Josh. Josh was rendered unconscious. When Nadine returned home, Mack told her if she called the police he would make her watch while he killed the rest of the children. Instead, Nadine watched while Josh slowly died. They buried Josh in the basement crawl space and told his siblings that he'd gone to stay with his father's family. Nadine and Mack were arrested when school officials questioned Josh's whereabouts and alerted the police, who ultimately found his body. Mack pled guilty to murder and received a fifteen-year mandatory sentence. Nadine went to trial and was sentenced to twenty-five years for her role in hiding and failing to prevent the crime.

When we interviewed Nadine the first time, her wishes for the future focused on love. She said she did not know what was stronger, a mother's love or God's love, but one of her wishes was that everyone could know the joy and happiness of God's love. She also wished that everyone could grow up happy and healthy and loving one another, "like it says in the Bible."

Celina

When we first interviewed Celina, she said she had been trying to focus on the good times she had growing up, when her family would travel. That was before her father started drinking and doing drugs. After that she mostly remembers him tearing up the house and beating her mother and all the children. Celina said she still has visions of him "pounding her in the face." She recalled that on one occasion, after she and her siblings had worked in the hot sun all day, her father still demanded more work. When her sister refused, Celina's father beat her so badly that she was hospitalized for two months. When Celina was about eight, her uncle began sexually abusing her until "I knew better."

Celina identifies an experience she endured at age seventeen as a turning point in her life. She was attacked by a gang of adolescents and spent months in the hospital recovering. After this attack, she had what she described as fits of rage and post-traumatic stress disorder. Celina became involved in a relationship and had four children; eventually, however, the relationship became abusive and she left her partner and moved to another city.

Celina's seven-year-old daughter, Sabrina, had been having difficulties in school since kindergarten. She was expelled from several schools for behaviors ranging from stealing from the teachers to hitting other children. Celina also reported that at home Sabrina would "cut up things like the sofa, play with the dog's private parts, and take food out of the refrigerator and line it in rows." Celina later learned Sabrina was being molested by her grandfather.

Celina said that during the whole time she had children she never "whooped" them; she tried to punish them by taking away privileges. She did not want to repeat the "generational curse" of child abuse. With Sabrina this tactic did not work, she said, and Celina began to punish her with "licks" on her hand. Eventually she progressed to "licks" on the backside.

A single parent with four young children, Celina began to drink excessively. Several times, she called a community organization to ask for help, but she never followed through with a support program. The night before Sabrina died, Celina called her mother and told her that "something strange is going on with me." Then she spent the night drinking. In the morning, a teacher came to Celina's home to discuss Sabrina's behavior. After the teacher left, Celina began to punish Sabrina. Celina said she doesn't remember exactly what happened, but she had visions of being attacked by the gang of adolescents. The next thing she remembers is Sabrina lying on the ground sleeping. Later that day, friends came over and Celina began drinking again. Eventually she realized that Sabrina was not waking up. She took her to the hospital but it was too late, and Sabrina was pronounced dead.

Since she has been in prison, Celina has embraced Christianity. She said she talks to Sabrina every day. Perhaps most important, she feels that she has broken the "generational curse" (abusive patterns) and that her life and her children's lives will be alright because she is "paying for the sins of her fathers."

Julie

Julie's sister was born on Julie's first birthday. Shortly after that, Julie's mother began drinking heavily and her father left home, leaving no forwarding address. When Julie was two, her grandparents came to her mother's home to visit and found there was no food in the house and the children were playing on the roof. They reported her mother to the state Child Protective Services. Julie's mother lost custody due to neglect, and Julie and her sister were placed in foster care. They remained there until Julie was five, when they were adopted as a sibling set.

Julie's adopted parents expected her to "watch over" her sister. Her adoptive father ran the local chapter of Big Brothers/Big Sisters and Julie maintains that he cared more for those kids than he did for her or her sister, acting primarily as a disciplinarian with them. She describes herself as a good child, however, who never got into trouble. She said she cooked, cleaned, and did her homework. Julie said her childhood wasn't that bad, but that the only time she was happy was when she was with her grandmother.

Julie had her first child when she was twenty-one. She said the father of her child was never interested in him and tried to fake paternity tests in order to avoid child support. Eventually Julie had three more children, all by separate fathers.

Julie was living with the father of the last child when a fire broke out in their home and three of the children perished. It is unclear to her how the fire started. She maintains it could have been that the children were playing with matches or that perhaps her boyfriend left a cigarette smoldering in the bedroom. Julie was the only adult in the home when the fire started. All the children were upstairs and she was downstairs. She did not go upstairs to attempt to save them. She wondered aloud about why her surviving child, who was ten, had not managed to save the younger children.

Julie was convicted of fatal child neglect in the deaths of her three children.

Marlene

Marlene describes herself as having been a "holy terror" while growing up. She said she was diagnosed with attention-deficit hyperactivity disorder when she was in kindergarten and has been medicated for it her whole life. Marlene was three years old when her parents divorced. When she was seven, her life changed dramatically. Her father, whom Marlene called a "career criminal," was incarcerated, and Marlene's mother married her biological father's half brother. Suddenly there was a new man and soon after a new baby, and in retrospect, Marlene notes that the transition was difficult for everyone. Despite the fact that she did not get along with her stepfather, she said no one hurt or abused her, and all in all it was a good childhood. She said she and her stepfather largely ignored each other.

As an adolescent Marlene was "always in trouble," though not with the legal system. She also reported she was never interested in drugs or alcohol because they made her feel out of control. Most of her "trouble" seems to revolve around breaking the rules around the house. By nineteen she had a daughter, and fifteen months later she had another daughter, Dakota, by a different father. She was still living with her parents at that time, and everyone agreed that Marlene should relinquish Dakota for adoption. After one week, Marlene changed her mind and retrieved the infant from the adoptive parents.

Marlene said her mother was tired of having to take care of Marlene and her babies, so she helped Marlene to secure her own home in a public housing project. Marlene described this time period as follows: "I wouldn't say I was a terrible parent, but I wasn't a good parent. I am too scatterbrained. I don't think about things a lot. I wasn't abusive but I was neglectful. I would give them a cup of Cheerios and have them go about their business. There were things I should have done more that I didn't. . . . The house was always a mess and I didn't care. . . . I didn't pay much attention to the kids." Marlene stated she just wanted to be a teenager, not a parent.

It is unclear how Dakota died. Marlene asserted that the baby had something bad in her and was destined to die. "She wasn't your average baby," she said. "She didn't sit up, wasn't mobile, and didn't cry. It was almost like she wasn't there." Marlene seldom referred to Dakota by name, and she adamantly denied allegations by the state that Dakota died from severe neglect, let alone from any intentional harm on her part. "I did not cause harm to the child purposely or even accidentally," she said.

Patty

Patty describes her childhood as chaotic. Her mother was an alcoholic, there was constant arguing, her uncles often would fight in the yard, and "it was not unusual to see someone passed out on the steps." Patty mentioned that she had been molested when she was five but did not want to provide details because it was "over for her, in the past." She became pregnant in seventh grade, had her first child when she was fourteen, her second at fifteen, a miscarriage at sixteen, and her third child at seventeen. While she was pregnant with her third child, Patty's mother also found out she was pregnant. Because her mother was an alcoholic, Patty cared for her own children and also for her mother's new baby.

Patty had a turbulent relationship with Frankie, the father of her first three children. When she became pregnant, Frankie moved in with Patty and her mother. Although she was only thirteen, and he was nineteen, Patty's mother allowed Frankie to live with them. Frankie hit Patty, even at the start of their relationship, and when he lost his job and money became scare, he became more abusive. Patty's mother knew that Frankie was beating Patty, and occasionally she told him to leave. She always changed her mind, though, and permitted Frankie to return.

Eventually, Patty left Frankie and her mother's home and moved out to marry a man named Bill. Patty described Bill as a good provider and father but said he "sucked" as a husband. Bill and Patty had one child, Vicky. After Vicky's birth, Patty began using drugs and alcohol and says that she began to go out and "party" at every opportunity that arose. She said she would be with the kids during the day and then party all night. After a year or so, Bill, who did not drink or take drugs, became tired of this life and they divorced. Patty recalls that she felt like she "was a no good mom addicted to drugs," so she decided to kill herself by driving into a telephone pole. Although she was seriously injured, she did not die, and she used the recovery time in the hospital to gain some control over her addictions.

When she recovered, she moved back in with Frankie, and when things deteriorated, she reunited with Bill. Neither of these arrangements was sustainable, though, so Patty and her children moved into a dilapidated apartment on their own. In order to provide a "roof over their heads," one of Patty's brothers moved in with her, and Patty was able to afford to have the utilities turned on. Patty describes her entire family as either alcoholics or drug abusers; her brother was no exception. She recalled that he drank heavily and routinely would pass out on the floor of their apartment.

One night after her brother had passed out from drinking, Patty wanted to continue to party. She left her brother in her apartment with her children and went across the hall to see if her new neighbor, Rick, wanted to have a drink. Rick agreed, and they drank until they passed out. When she awoke in the morning, her daughter was missing. After the police found Vicky's body, Rick maintained that he and Patty had been drunk and had killed Vicky together. Patty rejected this accusation and maintained that Rick alone had killed Vicky. Patty was nonetheless convicted.

Patty said Child Protective Services frequently had been alerted to conditions within her home, and although she had been investigated, she never lost custody of the children. When asked during the second interview how incarceration has affected her, Patty said, "I've matured, grown, and learned how to be a different type of mother. Before I felt that as long as we had a room, food in our bellies, and clean clothes on our backs, I was a good mother. Now I think you need love, emotional support, and good communication. And I don't believe in spanking anymore."

Vanessa

Vanessa's mother was fifteen years old when Vanessa was born. Vanessa never mentioned her father except to say that she was his only child. Another man fathered her four younger siblings. When Vanessa was old enough, she helped with most of the responsibilities of the house, including raising her siblings. She stated, "They were like my own kids growing up." Vanessa did not "figure out" that her mother and stepfather were doing drugs until she was a teenager.

Vanessa became pregnant when she was fourteen years old but concealed the pregnancy and eventually went into labor at a family gathering. The baby was born prematurely but survived, and by the age of eighteen Vanessa had three children and was living with the father of the two youngest children. The relationship was abusive, and Vanessa recalls that they were continually separating and then getting back together. Vanessa said she only smoked marijuana or drank when she was with her boyfriend. She supported herself and her children with monthly public assistance, which she supplemented with income from selling crack cocaine. She said that she never used the drug but that selling it helped her to afford to buy nice things for her children and to achieve some power in her neighborhood.

Vanessa indicated she was not abused as a child but that she did "get her ass whipped." She said she also whipped her children when they needed to be disciplined, but that because they were young she did not hit them with an extension cord or a switch, as her mother had done to her. Instead, she used a belt. During one incident, Vanessa's oldest daughter taunted her by saying she was going to tell her father that Vanessa's boyfriend beat Vanessa and the children, so Vanessa whipped her. The child's arm broke when she hit the wall. Instead of taking her to the hospital, Vanessa "set" her daughter's arm. Vanessa said she did not take her child to the hospital for fear that she would lose custody to the state. Eventually, when the state Department of Child Protection learned about the incident, Vanessa lost custody. She served a short jail term, and had to complete parenting classes before she could regain custody.

One year later, Vanessa's youngest daughter died. The cause of death remains uncertain. In the days prior to her death, Vanessa's daughter suffered a burn when she was scalded with hot water. The circumstances of the burning incident also are unclear. Vanessa did not believe that the burn required medical attention so she did not bring the child to the hospital. Two days later, when Vanessa could not wake up her daughter, she called paramedics, but by the time they arrived, the child was already dead. Vanessa vehemently denies the claim, made by the prosecution at her murder trial, that she strangled her child. Instead, she believes that her daughter died of an infection related to the scalding.

During both interviews Vanessa indicated that with all the abuse in her relationship with her boyfriend, it was inevitable someone would have been hurt. During her second interview, she told us that not a day goes by that she doesn't think about her daughter. Crying, she told us, "You learn from your mistakes and pay for those mistakes."

2

"She's the World to Me"

The Mother-Daughter Relationships Described by Mothers Who Committed Filicide

MOTHERING IS SOMETHING that, to a great extent, women learn from their own mothers. Experts ranging from psychoanalysts to biologists concur in their opinion that mothers serve as role models for their daughters, setting norms and expectations that inform their daughter's sensibilities about what it means to be a mother.[1] Accordingly, we were quite curious to know what mothers who had killed their children thought about their own mothers.

Interestingly enough, we did not need to ask questions; instead, in the majority of our interviews, before we even asked, these women spoke of their connections to their mothers and of the centrality of their mothers in their own lives, both as children and today. Even a generic question, such as "What was going on in your life at the time of your crime?" was likely to elicit a long description of the connection, or more often, the tension between the woman and her mother.

The central role that the women ascribed to their mothers stood in stark contrast to the far more peripheral roles played by their fathers. Some of the women we interviewed did not know, or scarcely knew, their biological fathers. Indeed, many of the women's biological mothers and fathers separated when the women were small children. In the few cases in which the women's parents stayed together, the women seldom mentioned their fathers when describing their lives. When they did mention them, typically it was to make a passing reference to "my parents" or to describe deeply troubling stories of abuse at their fathers' hands — stories that are discussed in chapter 3.

The more common male authority figures in these women's childhoods were their mothers' boyfriends and new husbands — those who served as stepfathers to these women. As with their stories about their biological fathers, the least troubling stories about their stepfathers were those in which the woman and her mother's partner tolerated and ignored one another. More often, the relationship between these women and their mother's partners was fraught with rivalry and abuse.

The stories these women told when asked about family and childhood largely were stories about their mothers. In discussing their mothers, the women's comments paid tribute to two interconnected sensibilities: an undying desire to please their mothers and also a keen awareness of how vulnerable their mothers made them feel. These sentiments exist in a strange tension with one another. As one woman said, in the course of our first interviews, "I want to make my mom happy and proud of me for once." Just as common was the feeling expressed by another woman, also in the first set of interviews: "My mother, she has this thing where she can hurt me and no one else can."

The intertwining of a yearning for approval with a keen sense of vulnerability permeates these women's stories about their mothers. This combination is not truly unusual; indeed, it is consistent with observations about the centrality of motherhood made by various theorists and experts. Noted biologist Sarah Blaffer Hrdy observed, "For species such as primates, the mother *is* the environment, or at least the most important feature in it during the most perilous phase in any individual's existence."[2]

What is perhaps most interesting about these women's stories about their mothers is that they maintained their connection to them in spite of the fact that the environments they provided were so unsafe. Poet and social commentator Adrienne Rich writes eloquently of the connection between a mother's life and a daughter's inheritance: "The quality of the mother's life — however embattled and unprotected — is her primary bequest to her daughter, because a woman who can believe in herself, who is a fighter, and who continues to struggle to create livable space around her, is demonstrating to her daughter that these possibilities exist."[3]

The women with whom we spoke described their mothers as having struggled mightily to create "livable space" and having, more often than not, subordinated their daughters' needs in their quest for stability. Rich goes on to note that "the first knowledge any woman has of warmth, nourishment, tenderness, security, sensuality, mutuality, comes from her mother."[4] The stories we heard contained scant reference to warmth and nurturing. Instead, the women with whom we spoke told sad, disturbing, and frightening tales about their relationships with their mothers. For the most part, they could not rely on their mothers as sources of unconditional, consistent love and comfort.

The stories we heard were replete with pain and disappointments, small and large. Their mothers permitted them to be abused by others. They beat them. When they fought, their mothers said horrific things to them, encouraging them to feel unwanted and unloved. Their mothers stayed in abusive relationships, they tolerated being beaten and humiliated, and they let their daughters' boyfriends beat and humiliate them. When the fighting escalated, the mothers routinely chose their male partners over their daughters, sometimes forcing their daughters from their homes. On occasion, they left their daughters behind them, hoping to begin a new life elsewhere.

In view of the relatively negative nature of these relationships, it was surprising to us that, rather than working to cut their mothers out of their lives, these women remained intensely attached to them. Sometimes, the relationships they described seemed to be one sided, in that their mothers remained absent, and the women seemed to be invoking their potential, rather than their actual mothers. In other cases, though, these women had cultivated real connections with their mothers, forgiving them their shortcomings, and in turn being forgiven for having killed their mother's grandchild.

In spite of the occasionally seismic scale of suffering experienced by these women in their relationships with their mothers, the texture of these relationships was surprisingly familiar to us. Even when we felt astonished by the level of dysfunction or cruelty that these women endured at their mothers' hands, we also recognized their emotional responses as similar in some ways to our own. The similarity lies in the intertwined yearning for approval and vulnerability to judgment and pain. A mother can cut her daughter to the core with merely a glance or a particular inflection. From the daughter's perspective, there is no ambiguity in her gestures. But just as there is vulnerability to pain, so too is there joy in approval.

The boundaries between mother and daughter are porous, at best, making it hard to know the difference between what makes her proud of us and what makes us proud of ourselves. We understood the stories these women told about their relationships with their mothers; they were familiar to us not because we had lived them, but rather, because we had lived our own, which somehow were just similar enough.

Renowned psychoanalyst Nancy Chodorow describes the mother-daughter connection as cyclical: "The reproduction of mothering begins from the earliest mother-infant relationship in the earliest period of infantile development. . . . [P]eople's experience with their early relationship with their mother provides a foundation for expectations of women as mothers."[5] From this perspective, it is vital that we start our inquiry into the lives of women who killed their children by considering the stories they told about their own childhoods and, in particular, about their own mothers. It was clear from their stories that the relationships between our interviewees and their mothers changed over time. We spoke with the women we interviewed about their evolving relationships with their mothers, beginning with early childhood and moving through their lives to the present.

Early Childhood Experiences

More than half of the women we interviewed grew up without the presence of their biological fathers in their lives, let alone in their homes.[6] For the most part, their early years were spent in single-parent households. Although we did not ask the women how old their mothers were when they were born, their stories speak to a high level of instability in their family lives. It seems likely that these women were born to relatively young mothers, and it is clear that, at least during their early childhoods, a considerable amount of their mothers' energy was devoted to pursuing romantic relationships.

Interestingly, none of the women blamed or even resented their mothers for having forged new relationships. Even Nadine, whose mother relinquished custody, moved to a different state, and left her two young children with an abusive, violent father, did not begrudge her mother for her choices: "My mom met a man with kids and took care of them like us. . . . She is my picture of a good mother. Always loving. She loved me no matter what I did. . . . My mother explained that she would leave me with [my father] because she didn't have the money to take care of us. She moved to another state with my stepfather."

When their mothers found new partners, the women we interviewed typically became members of blended households, in which they were raised by their biological mothers and their stepfathers. This dynamic often generated a feeling of outsider status, particularly after their mothers gave birth to more children — half siblings — with their new partners.

Years before Nancy found herself homeless, with a toddler and a newborn baby, she was aware of her "outsider status." She was raised with four half siblings, and she described her childhood experience in a way that typified many of the stories told by the women with whom we spoke: "I was the black sheep, the oldest, and wasn't dad's 'real daughter,' as were my two sisters. His side of the family was verbally and physically abusive to me. Grandma hit me with brushes until they broke. Mom physically abused me and even laughed about having thrown me at the wall, when talking about it years later with my aunt."

Likewise, Marlene, who at the time of her crime was living alone, longing to be a teenager, and struggling to care for her two young babies, wistfully described the way that her life as a child changed when her mother remarried. Marlene was her mother's oldest and only child until she reached age seven. She describes herself as having been "[a] bad kid" and explains that her attention-deficit hyperactivity disorder made her hard to control. Given this problem, Marlene noted that her mom "[d]id the best she could; better than I would've done." But, she says, "Childhood was stressful by age seven. Mom married and had a husband and a new baby right away." Marlene believes that because her new stepfather was also Marlene's biological father's half brother, her stepfather hated her and never wanted her around him.

One of the most painful aspects about being the family outcast, as described by so many of these women, is that the outcast alone is blamed for disrupting the family. Even in the retelling of their stories, the women seemed to accept that they were the cause of family strife, and they spend little time wondering about the things that might have provoked their objectionable behavior or about the proportionality of the punishment they received. One of the women we interviewed related this story: "Mom had a new boyfriend that I didn't like so I acted out a lot. She put me in some place at Ohio State University where I used to get shots a lot and I couldn't function. I was dizzy and I ran into walls. My sister remembers coming to visit me; . . . my mom denies that I was drugged at all, but I remember it. I think I was there for about a month. She told me I could come home if I could get along with her boyfriend."

In several cases, the women described being emotionally, and in some cases, literally abandoned by their mothers. One of the women with whom we spoke was abandoned by her mother at eighteen months. Her mother left her with a babysitter and moved to another state with her new boyfriend. She was placed in foster care, and her mother eventually was arrested, convicted of child endangerment, and served six months in prison. A more common pattern was that of substance abuse on the part of the mothers, which entails a figurative rather than a literal abandonment.

For example, recall Vanessa's story. At age ten, she was the oldest of five children. Her mother and her stepfather were drug addicts. As a result, they were absent from home for long periods of time and often not available to their children even when they were physically present. Vanessa's status as the oldest, and also as the only child not fathered by her stepfather, meant that she was held responsible when anything went wrong during her parents' absence. She described scenarios in which her mother and stepfather would return from partying and find that a sink was broken or that a doll had melted because the girls had tried to use a curling iron to fix her hair. Vanessa explained that incidents like this routinely triggered severe beatings.

Many of the women spoke about the interpersonal violence in their childhood homes. As is often the case with households that experience domestic violence, the violence between spouses carries over to the children.[7] Experts estimate that almost 50 percent of children of battered women are abused.[8] Even those children who are not beaten do not escape harm. Studies confirm that children in physically violent families are more likely to have social, psychological, and academic problems than children who do not witness or experience such violence.[9]

Many of the women with whom we spoke described themselves as victims of this "spillover violence." Consider the description of childhood patterns provided by one of the women: "My childhood was pretty abusive. My mother was an alcoholic and my stepfather abused my mother. He had two kids of his own and she had two kids and I guess we were the devils and his kids were angels. She stayed and every time he beat her she would drink. The abuse started when I was about 10 and I tried to protect my mother because I loved her. I couldn't stand to see her getting beaten like that. So the more he beat her the more she drank."

In spite of the instability caused in their lives, both by virtue of their mothers' alcoholism and also by the abusive intimate relationships in which their mothers remained, the women we interviewed professed loyalty and compassion for their mothers. This loyalty is particularly remarkable in view of the extent to which their stories describe mothers who were inconsistent sources of support, let alone love.

For instance, the following describes one woman's childhood relationship with her mother and is typical of many of the stories we heard:

> My mom would go through DT's [delirium tremens] and I always said that I didn't want to be like that. I took care of her like she was a child. I had a lot of responsibility. Maybe my actions came from her — she would leave for weeks at a time drinking. It was like my childhood was over . . . that I went straight to adulthood. I don't blame my mother . . . she was basically doing the best that she could. I don't think that that is what she wanted with her life — to choose to be with an abusive man and drink. I think she loved us unconditionally and that's how my children feel about me.

Adolescence and Separating from Mom

Given that adolescence is thought to be a challenging developmental phase, even for those who come from relatively stable, loving families, it is no surprise that the stories these women told about their relationships with their mothers during their teenage years were filled with strife. The major developmental task of adolescence involves growing apart from and independent of one's parents, so that one is able to function as an autonomous adult in society.[10] The stories told by our interviewees, the vast majority of whom became mothers when they were adolescents,[11] build on the descriptions of instability that marked their early childhoods. Typically, one thinks of the turbulence of mother-daughter relationships during adolescence as resulting from the dramatic changes in the girl, as she moves through puberty and into adulthood. In these women's lives, however, the instability in their relationships with their mothers seemed to derive at least as much from their mother's unreliability as from their adolescent rebellion.

The adolescent world described by many of these women is unsafe and even violent. It is also surprisingly lonely, given the number of other people in their immediate families. At least in retrospect, these women describe themselves as longing for their mothers' love or at least for their attention. This longing was quite natural given their mothers' distraction and indifference to them. Indeed, the combination of violence and the longing for affection likely helps to explain the relatively young age at which these girls became mothers themselves.

The Violence

Those interviewees who came from physically abusive homes spoke of the escalation in violence as they moved into adolescence. For instance, consider Nancy's life at home, prior to the instability and eventual home-lessness that she experienced after the birth of her babies. The abuse that Nancy endured when her mother remarried and had four children with her new husband did not diminish as Nancy grew older. Instead, Nancy said that her mother beat her routinely or "whenever she had a bad day." "I was nineteen and a half years old [and the mother of two children] when I got my last whipping. She had me bend over the table and whipped me. I was nineteen and a half. That should tell you something," she said. Nancy described a suicide attempt she made at age seventeen, when she still was living with her mother. After a particularly difficult fight with her mother, she swallowed a bottle of Anacin and drank Windex. This suicide attempt failed because she vomited. Then, when she was eighteen years old, her mother yelled at her, saying, "When are you gonna get outta my life?" Nancy described what happened next as follows: "I went into her room and grabbed a gun and shot [at herself], but there were no bullets. She called 911. They arrived, and asked, 'Why would a beautiful girl like you do this?' I answered, 'My mom told me to.' They asked my mom, 'Is this true?' 'Yes,' she answered, 'and would you take her somewhere so I don't have to clean up the blood stains when she does?'"

The beatings that these women described having endured as small children did not necessarily dissipate as they grew older and bigger. One of the women spoke of the power that her mother had over her in the following story:

> She did the best she could but I don't understand why people abuse their children and say mean things to their children. She used to tell me I was ugly, I was a bitch. When I was younger I didn't understand that I could be my own person. She controlled my mind. And so abu-sive — I have a false tooth because of her. She took my head and put it against the kitchen counter. Those people you can call when you are abused — I was seventeen and she had really long nails and put them down my face — [because] I wanted to get pizza with my friends.

My girlfriend took me to her mother's house and it was documented.
I wish I knew that when I was younger. She made me feel this big
[showed with fingers] like a monster standing over a little person. Even
when I got a job she took half my paycheck so I could never leave. She
would ask why I wouldn't get my own apartment but she wouldn't give
me any money. She was a trip — she really was. Very controlling. Basically, I have never been so scared of a person in my life as my mother.
I hated her — just because of what she put me through. I didn't do
drugs — I wasn't a bad person. I had a job. I did whatever she told me
to do. I remember this one time when this guy asked me out — like
when I was junior or senior in high school. He said, "I'll come get you
at noon," and I was so scared that I wouldn't even ask her.

Many of the stories of child abuse that the women told us included
sexual as well as physical abuse. Indeed, nineteen of the twenty-six women
who mentioned the abuse they suffered as children noted that they were
abused sexually as well as physically. Childhood sexual abuse carves a path
through the adult lives of those who survive it. We discuss the legacy of
this abuse as it pertains to the intimate relationships in these women's lives
in the next chapter of this book. It is also important to note the pernicious
impact that sexual abuse has on the relationship between the daughter,
who endures the abuse, and the mother, who in so many of these women's
lives knew of the abuse but failed to take steps to stop it.

As Professor Lynne Henderson notes, despite its relatively commonplace nature, there is a surprising silence surrounding the actual experience of child abuse, particularly child sexual abuse: "Child sexual abuse
is a form of furtive violence committed against vulnerable individuals. . . .
Awareness of the existence of sexual abuse of children is too painful and
too threatening to encounter unmediated; hence, fully understandable responses include shrinking away from thinking about it, explaining it away,
or flatly denying its existence."[12]

Among the women with whom we spoke, one of the most complicated and disturbing legacies of the sexual abuse they endured involved
their struggle to understand their mothers' abandonment of them to abuse
at the hands of others. This description from our first set of interviews is
typical:

I thought it was ok. Recently, I've been having flashbacks, nightmares,
and they're getting really bad so I have been talking to a counselor.

He told me that it would be a good idea to ask my mom. She denied it. Then she finally admitted to a lot of it. It was physical and sexual abuse from the time I was three to twelve. I had a military childhood and everything was covered up. It was like I had a picture perfect family. I have four younger sisters and my mom is divorced from the man who did this. My counselor said that I probably blocked things out because it was too painful. I am trying to deal with it but there are a lot of things I don't remember. I was a spoiled child, though, and I was taken care of very well.

There is a deep poignancy in the manner in which this woman struggles to reconcile her sense that she was well cared for, and even loved, with the fact that she was abused. She describes her mother as initially denying the fact of her abuse, even though she has since divorced the man who was the perpetrator of the abuse. The fact that the woman concluded her discussion of the subject by recalling that she was "a spoiled child," who was "taken care of very well," points to the difficulty she has in condemning her mother for permitting the abuse to occur, over the course of nine long years in her daughter's life.

In Patty's case, her alcoholic mother permitted Patty's nineteen-year-old boyfriend, Frankie, to move into their home when Patty was only thirteen. From the beginning, Frankie beat her. Patty felt powerless to stop the violence, and her mother's protection was inconsistent at best. On occasion, when Frankie beat Patty, her mother would "throw him out." The exile did not last long, though, and according to Patty, her mother "always let him move back in." Indeed, as the years passed, Patty's attempts to leave this man were foiled on several occasions because her mother permitted him to return to their home.

What is striking about these cases is not simply that these women experienced a considerable amount of violence at home but also that their mothers turned a blind eye to the violence their daughters were experiencing. Consider Nadine's story, in which she had five children by two violent, abusive men, the second of whom killed her son, Josh. When she was just ten years old, Nadine's mother left her and her younger brother in the custody of her abusive husband and moved to a distant state with another man. It seems implausible that her mother was unaware of her daughter's perilous situation before she left. Indeed, Nadine commented that her mother left her father because "he was abusive." That Nadine's father routinely raped and beat her should not have come as a surprise to her mother, but Nadine was not able to seek her mother's protection from him — when she moved away, her mother left no phone number, no address, and no means for her daughter to reach her. As was the case with many of the women with whom we spoke, Nadine expressed no resentment toward her mother for failing to protect her from harm. Recall that she said, "She is my picture of a good mother."

Although she describes a much more violent relationship with her mother, Nancy is similarly forgiving when it comes to her mother's willingness to sacrifice her daughter in order to protect her relationship with her male partner. Recall that Nancy was the oldest of five children in her home and the only one who was not fathered by the man with whom her mother was living. The manner in which she felt singled out for abuse, and the violence she experienced at home led her to repeatedly run away. "By age thirteen, I was out of the house," she stated. But she never stayed out for long. Instead, she continually returned to her mother's home, which was "not a safe space, but it seemed normal. Mom was yelling, and neighbors and family knew, but beating was normal."

During the course of a fight with her mother, when she was fifteen, her mother told her that she had not been fathered by the man she called "Dad" and that her biological father lived nearby. Two years later, Nancy arranged to meet her father, and soon after, she ran away to live with him. Nancy described their reunion obliquely, looking at the floor, as "a waste of time." She recalls that her father had her share a bed with him and that he kept telling her, "You look just like your mom did." He told her that he could not help but see her that way because, "for him and her two half brothers, they saw her as a 'lady' rather than as their daughter or sister because she hadn't grown up there."

There is a puzzle in the fact that, in spite of her description of a violent relationship with her mother, and a feeling that she was not welcome in her home, it took Nancy two years to contact her nearby father. Later, when she ran away from her father's house, she ran back to her mother's. Her mother did not protect her from the abuse of others, and indeed, by Nancy's account, frequently abused Nancy herself. At the end of the day, it seems that Nancy accepted the terms of their relationship, limited as it was.

The Loneliness

As they spoke of their transitions from early childhood into adolescence, many of the women we interviewed described themselves as caretakers for their younger siblings and often for their mothers. For instance, because her mother and stepfather were addicted to drugs, Vanessa describes herself as having "grown up fast," as she assumed the role of de facto caretaker for her four younger half siblings. Her predominant concern, as she recalls her childhood, was hiding her parents' drug use from everyone, including the only reliable adult in her life — her grandmother. "I always wanted to make it normal, to keep it so that things seemed normal," she said.

Perhaps as a result of this task, Vanessa did not describe herself as having had friendships of any sort. She seemed, instead, to be isolated within and continually preoccupied with her family. This isolation, coupled with the powerful wish to keep things "normal," likely contributed to her failure to tell anyone when, at age fourteen, she learned that she was pregnant. Instead, she carried the pregnancy in silence, never asking for help, until she was almost full-term. She went into labor in the bathroom of her grandmother's home, where the family had gathered to celebrate her mother's thirtieth birthday. Luckily, her relatives found her and took her and her newborn child to a hospital, where they both were treated.

Like Vanessa, Patty's household was crowded with family and relations — her boyfriend, her mother, and her younger siblings. Also like Vanessa, Patty's story speaks of a similar isolation and a yearning for emotional connection. As a seventh grader, Patty's life involved numerous responsibilities, including caring for her younger siblings, owing to her mother's alcoholism. Nonetheless, she described her response to learning that she was pregnant, at age fourteen, as being overwhelmingly positive. "I wanted to have a baby," she said. "I would be grown and always have someone who would love me."

In story after story, the women described themselves as being surrounded by circles of adult relatives, none of whom seemed to view her welfare as their concern. Instead, the girls were emotionally abandoned, so that even in households that were filled with other children and adults, there typically was no one who made them feel special or even loved. In light of this loneliness, it is little wonder that these women sought to create their own sources of love by having children of their own.

From Girls into Mothers: Relationships between Mothers and Daughters during the Pregnancy, Birth, and Infancy of Grandchildren

At the most fundamental levels, the experiences of pregnancy and child-birth are transformative. By virtue of the work associated with child rearing, for most women, the transformation is not completed when the baby is born; it is just beginning. In the exhausting weeks following the birth of a newborn, a father might wait impatiently for life to return to normal. For most mothers, it never does. There is no going back.

Economist Juliet Schor observed, in her book *The Overworked American*, that "mothers talk to her about sleep the way that someone who is starving talks about food."[13] But it is not merely sleep deprivation that marks the transformation wrought by motherhood. Nor is the work of motherhood challenging simply because it is work. And, contrary to popular expectations, it is not necessarily "instinctual."[14] Rather, what is uniquely challenging about mothering is that one can simultaneously love the work and hate it, yet there is little social support for giving voice to the feelings of despair and loathing that one might quite naturally feel. Poet and essayist Adrienne Rich pays tribute to the challenge of mothering, particularly for those new to the task:

> The physical and psychic weight of responsibility on the woman with child is by far the heaviest of social burdens. It cannot be compared with slavery or sweated labor because the emotional bonds between a woman and her children make her vulnerable in ways that a forced laborer does not know; he can hate and fear his boss or master, loathe the toil. . . . [For] the woman with children . . . [l]ove and anger *can* exist concurrently.[15]

Even a brief survey of the vast literature on pregnancy and childbirth gives testament to the wide range of physical, social, and emotional stressors associated with this transition.[16] Ideally, women can rely on the support and guidance of others when making the transition to motherhood. When one considers the lives of the women we interviewed, both during their pregnancies and, even more, during the early weeks of parenting their babies, one is struck by their isolation. They seldom had any physical, let alone emotional support from their families. None of the stories they told recounted their having received affection or special attention from their partners or from any of the adults in their lives in the early days and weeks after their babies were born. On the contrary, pregnancy further destabilized many of these women's connections with their families, and in particular with their mothers. Thus, not only were they left to traverse the journey into motherhood on their own, but more often than not, their journey was made more challenging by uncertainty about where they would live and whom they could trust to care for them.

Pregnancy

By their own description, many of the women we interviewed initially were somewhat pleased at the prospect of becoming mothers and eager for the life changes that their infants portended. In most cases, though, one could detect the panic that accompanied the joy in these women's responses to pregnancy. Almost all the women we interviewed were relatively young at the age of first pregnancy and were dependent on relationships that proved to be unreliable. Perhaps unsurprisingly, their mothers seemed to regard their daughters' pregnancies with ambivalence, expressing concern that their daughters were not yet able to care for a child and fear that they would be saddled with the burden of rearing their grandchildren. The result was that preexisting tensions between mother and daughter tended to escalate during pregnancy. This was even more true when the women became pregnant a second time.

Some of the women's families ignored their pregnancies and the changes they foreshadowed. The most striking example of ignoring a pregnancy is seen in the phenomenon of neonaticide, which involves the killing of a child within twenty-four hours of birth. Of the original forty women we interviewed, only two had committed neonaticide. In spite of this relatively small number, neonaticide occurs with surprisingly frequency. In appendix B we discuss the patterns surrounding neonaticide in greater detail and consider some of the reasons why there were not more neonaticide cases among the population of women we interviewed.

Laurie's story is typical of the phenomenon of neonaticide. Recall that she became pregnant as a result of having been raped by a friend of her stepfather and mother. She felt too ashamed to tell her mother and stepfather what had happened. Not only did Laurie resist disclosing her pregnancy to her mother or her stepfather, but also they claimed not to have noticed that she was pregnant.

The claim not to have noticed a daughter's pregnancy typically is taken at face value. On scrutiny, however, it seems less than fully credible and regardless, indicates a profound degree of isolation and silence in these family's interactions. It is difficult to mistake the large, rock-hard belly of a pregnant woman for that of one who is simply gaining weight. The claim that one did not notice that one's daughter was pregnant therefore implies not only that the parent did not recognize the emotional and the physical changes in their daughter over the course of the pregnancy, but also that they did not have much physical contact with her, particularly during the last five months or so of pregnancy. When we asked Laurie about what happened when her mother or other family members hugged her, she responded that no one hugged her. If they did notice anything, she said, they did not say anything about it.

The story of Vanessa's first pregnancy is quite similar. She was fourteen years old when she became pregnant for the first time. The father was a boy from school, whom she had known since kindergarten. She reports that she was "scared to death. I concealed [and] denied the pregnancy. I didn't believe in abortion. Grannie suspected it. I didn't say anything." Recall that Vanessa never acknowledged that she was pregnant and that she went into labor and delivered her baby at home, in the bathroom, during her mother's thirtieth birthday party.

Except for the fortuitous rescue by her aunt, Vanessa's story is similar to the neonaticide pattern. She blames herself for having refused to seek help, and yet, it is clear even from her own words (e.g., "Grannie suspected it") that the adults in her life knew, or should have known, that Vanessa was pregnant. After all, she was an eighth grader, in constant contact with her parents, her grandmother, and other extended family members. Vanessa's impending transition into motherhood threatened the precarious balance that permitted all the other adults in her life a degree of freedom. Acknowledging her pregnancy would also have meant coming to terms with the end of the status quo under which Vanessa essentially was responsible for raising her four younger siblings and for helping to conceal her parents' addictions. Thus, Vanessa endured her pregnancy alone.

It is difficult to imagine the terror that might lead a teenager to carry such a heavy secret, day after day, month after month. One of the women we spoke with described her actions as follows:

> I was afraid to tell my mom — I was seventeen and I didn't want to
> let her down so I kept it to myself. I told my grandmother and my

aunt about my pregnancy. No one else knew. I didn't get as big as normal women do. She was a big baby — eight pounds two ounces. It was
hard but I did it. . . . My mom asked me if I was pregnant and I said no.
I could've told her but I didn't. . . . I was afraid she would yell, scream,
say she hated me.

In spite of the fact that these young women had a range of legal options from which to choose when they learned that they were pregnant,
many of the women with whom we spoke ruled out abortion as contrary
to their family's values. Vanessa's story makes reference to such a conviction. So, too, did Marlene, who noted that, although her first pregnancy
was not planned, she did not consider abortion because "we don't do
that."

Several of the women whom we interviewed considered placing their
infants with an adoptive family. This decision is a challenging one for any
woman, and the literature on mothers who relinquish their babies speaks
to the fact that women who successfully do so typically receive an extraordinary amount of support, both from their families and from all those involved in the adoption process.[17] The family lives of the women we interviewed tended to be less supportive and more chaotic. Therefore it is
unsurprising that the women struggled with their impulse to relinquish
their babies. At some level, it felt not only "unnatural" but also perhaps
self-defeating, in that, for these women, a baby held out the promise of
a loving relationship; one that, in theory, could fill the emotional void in
these women's lives.

The women's mothers often expressed their ambivalence about their
daughter's impending motherhood by encouraging their daughters to relinquish their babies for adoption. For example, one of the women whom
we interviewed described the following interaction with her mother:
"When I had my daughter my mother talked me into giving her up for
adoption. So I signed and they gave me a couple of days to see. . . . I fell
into a deep depression. . . . I guess the look on her face and feeling in the
room. . . . I didn't want her to be somewhere else. My mother couldn't bear
to see me looking like that. There was a lot going on in the time [away]
from my baby."

Similarly, Marlene, who describes herself as having been a challenge
to live with owing to her attention-deficit hyperactivity disorder, struggled
with her mother over whether to place her baby with an adoptive family. Until her second baby was born, Marlene and her sixteen-month-old

daughter had been living with her mother, stepfather, and younger sister. Her mother had grown tired of having to "take care of everything for her." When she became pregnant a second time, a year later, her mom lost patience with her: "With number two, mom was sick of me, and kicked me out. I talked to Catholic Services and relinquished the baby for adoption. After birth, I stayed home with mom on the couch for a week, and then told mom I couldn't give my daughter away." Neither could her mother reconcile herself to housing and caring for both her daughter and her grandchildren. "There was no room in their house for me. My sister was thirteen. There were three bedrooms and I had two kids." So Marlene moved into an apartment, accompanied by her two children, a sixteen-month-old, and a newborn daughter.

One of the women with whom we spoke reported that her mother was so intent on her relinquishing her baby that she put her in a home for unwed mothers and had her lie and say the baby's father was unknown. In her recollection, none of the social workers or health care providers in this home attempted to ascertain her feelings about relinquishing the baby. Finally, just after the baby was born, she revealed the father's name, and he and his aunt assumed custody of the baby. Six months later, the mother reunited with the father and obtained custody.

To the extent that these women's families acknowledged their pregnancies, it seemed that they encouraged them to terminate them or to surrender their babies for adoption. The pregnant women tended to reject this advice, largely because they viewed their babies as a potential source of love. This struggle often compounded the stress on their relationships with their mothers or families. For example, consider the ways that Nancy's violent and turbulent relationship with her mother and her stepfather intensified when, at age nineteen, she became pregnant with her second child. Recall the painful stories that Nancy told about her family life prior to this point, including years of physical abuse by her mother, stepfather, and grandmother, failed efforts to run away to a better home, and suicide attempts. While hiding behind the couch one day, when she was several months pregnant, she heard her mom and stepdad arguing. "Either she goes or I do," said her stepfather.

Her mother chose her husband over her daughter, and Nancy went back to live with her biological dad, with whom she was forced to share a bed and to endure sexual abuse. After a particularly intense fight at her father's house, in which she punched and broke a screen, she ran away back to her mother's, leaving everything except for her thirteen-month-old son behind her. She delivered her daughter two or three weeks later. Within a week, she and her mother fought again, and her mother kicked her out, leaving Nancy and her two babies homeless.

The women said little about how they felt during their pregnancies. It seems self-evident that the experience of pregnancy, the inexorable, yet gradual transformation of one's body and one's life, must be shaped by the extent to which the pregnant woman feels secure in her surroundings. Many of the women whom we interviewed were unable to predict, with any degree of confidence, the manner in which they would live once their babies were born. The things about which they were uncertain were absolutely fundamental: Where would they live? How would they support themselves and their offspring? Who would take care of them? The only thing that most of them knew for certain was that their babies, when they were born, would immediately set into motion the end of their lives as they now knew them. For many of these women, the promise of change, even if uncertain, was preferable to the present.

Early Motherhood

For a mother, the early days, weeks, and months after a baby's birth typically are associated with extreme exhaustion, due in part to sleep deprivation, in part to recovery from childbirth, and in part to the challenge of adjusting to the demands, both literal and figurative, of motherhood. Ideally, women manage the transition into motherhood, or the adjustment to another child, by relying on the support and collaboration of others. Biologist Sarah Blaffer Hrdy observes that humans are not unique in this regard, noting that, from queen bees to elephants, many nonhuman mothers receive assistance in rearing their young. She maintains that our human ancestors also were "cooperative breeders" and speculates that one key to human well-being may lie in recognizing and honoring this aspect of our evolutionary heritage.[18]

In traditional cultures, new mothers are supported by their female relatives, who take care of them so that they, in turn, might devote themselves to caring for their newborns.[19] In contrast, in contemporary Western culture, the role of extended, and indeed of nuclear family has constricted to the point where it is not considered strange for new mothers to spend long hours alone with their baby, day after day. Few would argue, however, that it is ideal for a new mother to attempt to raise her child in isolation, without the support of a partner or family. This is all the more true when the mother is relatively young and unable to support herself.

One of the most consistent themes to emerge from the stories told to us by the mothers we interviewed was that of extreme isolation and vulnerability in the early weeks and months of their newborns' lives. The inherently problematic nature of this isolation was intensified by virtue of the fact that these women were so young and unsophisticated. To the extent that their mothers were present in their lives, they tended to ignore their daughters' struggles in coping with motherhood. Although most of these women maintained close relationships with their own mothers, seeing them weekly, if not daily, when it came to caring for their grandchildren, their mothers abandoned them to their own limited resources.

Nancy's story is perhaps the most vivid in terms of the isolation and lack of support she received following the birth of her children. Recall that she fought with her mother, and her mother kicked her out of her home shortly after the birth of her second child. Her daughter only lived for eleven weeks. In that short time, Nancy, her sixteen-month-old son and her newborn stayed in eleven different locations, including several stays in a homeless shelter. They spent no more than a few nights in any given place. "It was crazy," she said. "I left something behind at every place." The closest thing to support that Nancy received were the weekly visits from a nurse, called in by the Department of Social Services (DSS). The emotional connection that Nancy felt with her caseworker, which we discuss in chapter 6, was ironic, of course, because of the ostensibly punitive nature of that relationship.

Like Nancy, Marlene found herself displaced from her home in the immediate aftermath of giving birth to her second child. Recall that Marlene describes herself as having been "always in trouble," at least in part because of her attention-deficit problems. In addition, there were longstanding tensions between her and her stepfather. Everyone in her family agreed that it would be best if Marlene relinquished her newborn for adoption, but after a week, Marlene changed her mind. Her parents, however, were tired of having to take care of Marlene and her babies, so Marlene went to live in an apartment on her own, with two children.

The picture Marlene paints of life in that apartment is one of complete chaos. Her mother would visit her there, two or three times a week. Other than that, her only visitors were local teenagers, who came to hang out there when skipping school. They offered her no help in caring for the babies, and Marlene describes having been overwhelmed by the amount of work that the babies required. On a typical day, she said, "I would wake up, look at the television, notice the mess, and think about the need to clean, but I just didn't have energy. I just wanted to be a teenager, not a parent. I didn't want to be a parent. I didn't want to play with a sixteen-month-old boy. I'd rather give him Cheerios and have him watch television with me. I would dress him up and take pictures. Then I'd go back to being a teenager and doing what I wanted to do."

Although it is unfair to hold her accountable for her grandchild's death, one cannot help but wonder what Marlene's mother was thinking when she visited her daughter's home. By all accounts, it was filthy. Marlene's mother responded to the chaos in her daughter's life as one might imagine a parent responding to a child's messy bedroom. She stopped in, but looked the other way, rather than get involved in the struggle to keep things orderly. But in this case, the bedroom had two babies in it.

Even though the law typically does not require parents to provide support for, or even to protect their adult children, one cannot help feeling that, at some level, these women's parents were morally complicit in their grandchildren's deaths. In some cases, such as those involving alcohol or drug addiction, the women never had the consistent support of their parents in their lives. In many cases, though, the grandparents simply gave up on their daughters and on their grandchildren. They turned away as their daughters' worlds came apart. Their resignation seems understandable, if not excusable. They felt exhausted by their daughters' actions and by the complications set in motion with the births of their grandchildren. But it is obvious, at least in retrospect, that many of their daughters' decisions were set in motion by their own behavior as parents, fifteen or twenty years earlier.

The Bereaved Grandmothers: Reflections on the Relationship between Mother and Daughter in the Aftermath of Filicide

One interesting, if puzzling, theme that emerged from the stories these women told of their mothers was that they tended to describe their present relationships with their mothers as meaningful and positive ones. Furthermore, they understood the deaths of their own children as marking turning points in these relationships. This association, even if only partially true, is ironic in the extreme. It is as if the dead grandchild was some sort of scapegoat, whose death permitted those who survived to move forward, breaking old and toxic patterns, and forging new and more meaningful connections.

Consider Patty's story. Recall that Patty's mother's alcohol abuse dominated her childhood. From the age of thirteen, Patty's boyfriend, Frankie, lived with them, even though he beat her. After attempting to move across country with Frankie and their two small children, seventeen-year-old Patty returned home to her mother's house. At that point, Patty was pregnant with her third child. Her mother was pregnant as well and drinking heavily. Patty describes that period in her life without bitterness. Within a matter of months, she found herself caring for her own three children — a newborn and her two- and three-year-old sons — as well as for her new baby brother. In spite of the enormous challenge posed by this situation, she did not start "drinking or drugging," as she put it, until she was twenty-two years old — four or five years later. That, as she describes it, was the beginning of much of the trouble in her relationships with her children, as well as with their fathers.

When she was convicted of murdering her four-year-old daughter, Patty says that her mother "found religion." She stopped drinking and assumed legal custody of Patty's youngest child. Patty says that today she and her mother are "like friends." Her mother writes to her, and Patty feels like she's there for her. Although she has not visited her even once in the more than ten years that Patty has been in custody, Patty is not bitter. "She writes but can't come," says Patty understandingly. "The kids keep her going. [She's] been through too much."

Likewise, Nadine describes her relationship with her mother as having been rekindled at the time of her arrest. Recall that Nadine's mother had disappeared from her life when Nadine was only ten, when she left Nadine's abusive father, remarried, and moved out of state. Nadine saw her only once in the years between her departure and Nadine's arrest. When Nadine was charged with murder for having failed to seek medical assistance after her husband brutally beat her son, Nadine's mother came to see her in jail and to meet, for the first time, her surviving grandchildren. She attempted to secure legal custody of the children, but they were placed with their respective fathers' families instead. Nadine decried the court's rejection of her mother's petition for custody, expressing her belief that her mother should have been permitted to raise Nadine's children.

When describing her relationship with her mother today, Nadine spoke of her with generous praise. Although Nadine did not mention receiving visits from her mother, or even letters from her, Nadine spoke of her mother with love, noting that she was a true source of support in her life. Said Nadine, "She is my picture of a good mother: always loving."

Vanessa, too, described wistfully the loving bond forged with her mother in recent years. Vanessa, who spent much of her own childhood taking care of her younger siblings and hiding her mother and stepfather's substance abuse from other family members, found that, as an incarcerated adult, she could once again help take care of her mother. While Vanessa was already incarcerated for the death of her daughter, her mother was convicted of a drug-related crime. She was sent to the same prison that housed Vanessa, and Vanessa was able to "protect" her mom. She helped her to find safety within the prison culture and taught her how to take care of herself. "The caretaker role is what comes to me naturally," she said.

One might think that, to the extent that a mother-daughter relationship could grow stronger in the aftermath of such a tragedy as filicide, it would be owing to the mother finding some way to comfort her incarcerated daughter. These stories tell quite a different tale. Instead, it is the daughters, behind bars for having killed their babies, who end up providing their own mothers with comfort and solace. The story of one of the women, who wept throughout this part of our interview, testifies to that process:

> When I got locked up, my mother never wrote me. After six months, she sent me a Christmas card. I was on suicide watch. They gave me the mail and I started crying. And it must have been really bad. It must have said something really mean in it, I guess, because I started crying and they asked if I wanted any more mail from her again. . . .
>
> [M]y mom was more calm when she was drinking. I am not going to say she didn't look out for me. I had clothes, food, but no love. My aunt told me once I was so much like my mother — I look like her and she didn't want me to be like her but much better. She didn't do it to my brother or sister [abuse] but to me. I don't know what went on in her life. She writes me all of the time now. She feels lonely. I don't want her to feel that pain that she was that bad of a person even though she was. So, I write her and tell her, "you're not a bad person" — you did the best you could, but I don't understand why you did it to me. . . .
>
> I was in a prison — my mother's prison. . . . And right now, I really do feel free. I am not with my mom — in that prison.

Conclusion

It is difficult to reconcile these women's professed adoration for their mothers, the passionate way in which they speak of their connections to them, with the humble, limited nature of the relationships that their own stories depict. Simply put, their mothers were not, and are not reliable presences in their lives. They almost never come to visit their daughters, they seldom write, and typically, they are no more present as a source of support for their grown, incarcerated daughters than they were when their daughters were small children.

Indeed, it seemed that the women we interviewed felt a need to protect and forgive their mothers, explaining, and even justifying the ways in which their mothers had abandoned them. They were far less generous when it came to judging themselves; as we will see, their stories were filled with their own sense of shame and guilt for having failed to be good mothers.

It seems likely that there is an integral relationship between the tendency these women had to blame themselves and their inclination to forgive their mothers. To the extent that their mothers did not kill them, one might surmise that their mothers were, in fact, better mothers by comparison. And yet, in so many of these cases, their mothers not only failed to protect them, but they affirmatively placed them in harm's way. The fact that these women survived into adulthood seems, in most of these cases, to owe relatively little to the skill and devotion of their mothers.

The resistance that these women had to blaming their mothers might also be viewed as a healthy adaptive strategy. Blaming their mothers would trigger feelings of anger and even shame. Were they to accurately assess the extent to which their mothers had failed them, these women might come to feel, perhaps justifiably, that their mothers were at least partly to blame for the trajectory of their lives. Had their mothers taken even a marginally greater level of interest in them, their lives might have been redeemed. Perhaps they would not be in prison, and just maybe, their children might be alive today. Such feelings would be unproductive, at best, given the fact that, in any event, these women must continue to serve out their sentences. How much easier is it, then, to forgive them, taking all the blame onto themselves? "I was a bad kid," said Marlene. "I shouldn't never have had no kids, at that point, by myself. . . . My mom was there. But she'd dealt with me her whole life, so she'd just do things for me. I didn't have to do them, or learn to do them. . . . She did the best she could; better than I would've done."

In addition, acknowledging one's mother as flawed seems likely to trigger a degree of humiliation. Children feel ashamed of their parents' failings. Recall Vanessa's desperate struggle to hide her parents' addictions, and her yearning to make sure her family seemed "normal."[20] No one wants to admit that they are lacking something as fundamental as a mother's love. And so, no matter how badly they were treated, these women tended to love their mothers.

Nancy, who has worked closely with prison psychiatric services during the long years of her incarceration, reflected on the nature of her ties to her mother. Although her mother lives near the prison, Nancy has had only three visits from her in the ten years during which she has been incarcerated. She openly acknowledges the ways in which her mother was physically and emotionally abusive to her. And yet, she cries when speaking of her love for her mother and of how she still yearns for her mother's love. "I know it's sick," she says, "but she's the world to me."

3

Fighting for Love

Filicidal Mothers and Their Male Partners

THE STORIES OF women who kill their children necessarily start with stories about how they became mothers — with stories about sex, romance, and dreams of building a family and a future. The women with whom we spoke, however, did not tell their stories that way. Consistently, their relationships had been disappointing to them. Furthermore, so much had happened since the early days of their relationships with their children's fathers that they often viewed these relationships as a minor detail — a footnote — in their life stories. But to the extent that we seek to understand these women's stories, it is important to consider these relationships and the ways in which they helped to set in motion the later events in these women's lives.

Two of the most striking and troubling patterns in these women's lives emerge when one considers the role of love and intimacy in their relationships with men. First, virtually all the women we interviewed were teenagers, and often relatively young teens, when they became sexually active and, typically soon thereafter, pregnant. Second, most of their relationships with the men who fathered their children were marked by interpersonal violence and emotional abuse.

Dreaming of Romance

When asked about the timing of their first pregnancy, almost all the women we interviewed expressed the sense that both sex and pregnancy "just happened." They tended to describe themselves as passive recipients of male attention, as opposed to more active participants in "adult" behavior. In many ways, their behavior fits the normative, albeit antiquated, social script in which a woman's life both begins and ends when love finds her. Like Cinderella, romance (or at least sex) found these women, rather than the reverse. And once it found them, their lives were forever changed.

To the extent that they ascribed passive roles to themselves in their early intimate relationships, these women were by no means extraordinary. Indeed, the ample literature on the subject describes much of adolescent sexuality and pregnancy as spontaneous and unplanned.[1] For adolescents, sex typically "just happens," and as a result, particularly for newly sexually active teens, rates of contraception use are low.

Experts in adolescent psychology and moral development describe a common pattern of self-doubt among young teenage girls, whereby girls tend to look to others for validation, rather than asserting themselves and taking proactive steps to protect their needs.[2] The tendency to be passive and reactive is particularly true in girls' early (hetero)sexual encounters and likely is reinforced by several factors. First, although we live in a society in which premarital sexual activity is the norm,[3] there nonetheless remains a stigma associated with being prepared for, or expecting to have sex.[4] Thus a girl's use of contraception may be taken to mean that she wanted sex to happen and, as such, is somehow "easy," as compared to those for whom sex happened spontaneously.

Additionally, even when girls are sexually confident, the adolescent tendency to prioritize short-term factors over a careful consideration of long-term consequences leads many to engage in risky sexual behaviors.[5] For instance, a girl who finds it difficult to ask her partner to use a condom might assent to having unprotected sex, even though she knows that, in the long run, it increases her risk of sexually transmitted diseases or pregnancy.

More recent studies suggest that sexual mores may be shifting, permitting girls to embrace, or at least to pantomime, the role of sexual aggressor. Nonetheless, little has changed in terms of the social script regarding contraception. Girls may be increasingly permitted to acknowledge sexual desire, but stopping a sexual encounter to insure that they will be protected against unwanted pregnancy remains decidedly taboo. Instead, the sexual encounters described, even by girls who initiate sexual contact, often seem designed to maximize male pleasure and fail to take into account the one thing that insures that a heterosexual encounter will be strictly recreational for the female: contraception.[6]

Equally pernicious is the reported tendency of adolescents to value, or perhaps overvalue, connection and romance.[7] Reflecting on her past, one woman, who married an abusive man when she was sixteen and he was thirty, said, "I realized during my time with him it was not about love and if I had been in love, I wasn't anymore. I was probably more in love with the idea of being in love." Girls often romanticize their interactions with boys and men, and they interpret sexual overtures as evidence of love.[8] Their relative inexperience, coupled with a social script that encourages them to value connection to men as a mark of their maturity and desirability as a woman, leaves adolescent girls prone to exploitation and coercion. As a result, adolescent girls often assent to treatment by their male partners that more experienced women and men might find objectionable and unfair.[9]

For instance, consider Nadine's stories about her first significant relationship. After her parents divorced, ten-year-old Nadine and her brother lived on and off with her abusive father and her maternal grandfather. Neither man, according to her story, permitted her to rely on them as a parent. When she was fourteen years old, she became intimate with a seventeen-year-old named Johnnie and became pregnant with twins. Nadine describes their relationship: "At church I met Johnnie. I thought he was the greatest guy. One afternoon, while at his house, I started to miscarry. He was freaked out that nobody came to help me. I was covered in blood and a tissue ball was stuck to my panties. He was mad at his parents because they didn't get up to see what was the matter. He took me home. He didn't go in and show his rear end like I thought he would."

When pressed for details, Nadine tells the story of a very limited relationship with Johnnie, which consisted largely of her hanging out at his house and having sex with him. As is typical of early adolescents, she paid little attention to the long-term implications of her situation — such as what she would do, or what Johnnie was likely to do with her, once her babies were born. In her mind, her relationship with Johnnie was real. But when the relationship was put to a test — when Nadine began hemorrhaging and needed his help — he lacked the courage, or perhaps simply the commitment, even to accompany her into her grandfather's home.

Many of the stories these women told about their first sexual relationships resembled Nadine's. The women tended to believe they had found true love. They did not use contraception. They became pregnant. In spite of the relatively limited support they received from their partners, the women typically romanticized the nature of the relationship as a long-term, loving one and were therefore not overly troubled when they learned that they were pregnant.

For example, although she was living with her mother, stepfather, and four half siblings in a crowded home in which there was constant fighting and violence, Nancy recalled that she was thrilled to learn that she was pregnant with her first child. In spite of the fact that her boyfriend was also a teenager, unemployed, and living with his mother, she said, "the baby was planned. I loved his dad and wanted to be a mom. I was young. I was engaged. I was in love. I wanted to have his baby. He was violent, too, but never put his hands on me. I tried everything I could to get pregnant." By the time the baby was born, their relationship had ended.

As is often the case, in spite of the girls' dreams of having found true love, these early sexual relationships did not mature into long-term loving commitments. Instead, the boys often disappeared, particularly after the girls became pregnant. Even when the relationships endured, the presence of these men in the lives of these women during pregnancy and after the birth of their children often was sporadic and limited. Many of these women could not rely on their partners for even the most basic forms of economic or emotional support.

The law governing sexuality understands the vulnerability and risk of exploitation faced by young people in sexual relationships. For almost eight hundred years, the common law crime of "statutory rape" has attempted to protect girls (and in most states today, boys as well) from sexual exploitation by prohibiting sexual conduct with those under a legally established age of consent. In contemporary times, though, adolescent sexual activity is commonplace, and these laws tend to be enforced only in cases that prosecutors consider to be egregious.[10] Nor is it evident that the law could afford protection from sexual exploitation to young people, even if it were more routinely enforced.

The stories told by these women help depict the inherent limitations on the capacity of statutory rape laws to remedy the problems growing out of sexual encounters with young people. Even when they were disappointed in their relationships, or treated disrespectfully, these women did not see themselves as having been victimized. Nor did they find any injustice in the fact that they became pregnant and that their lives, but not their partners' lives, were permanently altered by the nonnegotiable demands that motherhood placed on them.

Instead, these women tended to describe their lives prior to having children as having been relatively aimless. They did not have plans that were derailed by virtue of becoming pregnant. They were not intent on a particular future; there were no hopes for graduation, let alone for college or a career, that were dashed by virtue of an unplanned pregnancy.

Love was supposed to be a new beginning. But the "love stories" they told were not part of an idealized script for romance. Instead, they often consisted of relationships that were, at their core, negotiated exchanges, such as that described by this woman from our first set of interviews:

> Our mom raised us that if we had sex with a man, they are supposed to take care of us. He cheated with a girl in his house. He took pictures of her . . . that didn't upset me because I knew he was cheating. . . . It was like a love thing — like breakfast in bed, he would make the bath water for me in the morning. He spent one hundred sixty dollars in groceries for me to fill up my fridge even though I had already shopped. Everything was OK.

Fighting for Love

Overview

Violence and emotional abuse stalked the intimate relationships described by the mothers who killed their children.[11] In most cases, the violence began early in their lives and came packaged with love, or what was purported to be love. Many of these women experienced sexual abuse as children — typically at the hands of their mothers and fathers, or their stepfathers.[12] As they grew into adolescence and began forming intimate relationships with others, the twinned packaging of sex and violence replicated itself. As one woman said, "One time I thought that if a man didn't hurt you that wasn't what it was supposed to be like." Many of the women did not discuss their relationships, but sixteen of the seventeen who did discuss the men in their lives indicated they were hit, beaten, yelled at, and intimidated by their boyfriends and husbands.

This fact should not surprise us. Researchers long have noted the grim commonality of prior abuse among incarcerated women.[13] Indeed, so common is the experience of intimate violence and emotional abuse among women in prison that domestic violence support groups are basic features of psychiatric service programs designed to serve this population. Many incarcerated women have, at some point in their lives, been subjected to violence at the hands of an intimate partner. Some speculate that this link is not merely coincidental, but rather, may be causal.[14] Women may be conditioned to accept violence from those whom they love, and their limited ability to distance themselves from abusive relationships seems, at least in some cases, to lead to their entanglement in criminal activities.

Knowing all this, we were not surprised to hear about the violence that marked the relationships between these women and the fathers of their children. At first, the violence that permeated the stories that these women told about their lovers seemed to congeal into a single story. These stories seemed to ratify the now-familiar descriptions of domestic violence articulated by experts and endorsed by those who work on behalf of battered women. Upon reflection, however, we found that, although the relationships were abusive, they were distinct. A more careful study of the stories told by the women with whom we spoke ratified Tolstoy's famous observation that while "all happy families resemble one another, each unhappy family is unhappy in its own way."[15]

A story told by one woman was particularly emblematic, for us, of the horror of domestic violence and the manner in which it might cause a woman's life to unravel. When she was sixteen, this woman ran away with a charismatic man who was twelve years older and much bigger than she was. Within a few months, she was pregnant and they married. She and her husband moved constantly, and he kept her isolated from family and friends. Over the next two years, as she had more children, her life became a continual struggle to evade her husband's violence: "Dealing with his alcoholism as a teenager — I didn't know how to keep my body between him and the kids. There were times I felt weak and insignificant but when I look back on them now, I was brave. He was a big man. And when he was angry, his anger and size was intimidating. He weighed three hundred pounds. I don't know how I did it." This woman tried to leave her husband several times before she finally escaped for good: "The last time I came back, my husband left me in Florida [with the babies]. Mom sent me a bus ticket — I told her not to send money because I knew he would spend it." After her escape, she and her children returned to her parents' home, and she began to attempt to pull her life together. She had managed to escape the cycle of violence and, over the course of the ensuing years, to come to terms with the terror and trauma that was the legacy of this terrible relationship: "Once I stopped being responsible for my husband, even my nightmares about him are not frequent or traumatic. [In my dreams] I am in control of him — I ask him to leave."

This woman's story resonated with us because it was familiar to us. Today, approximately 5.3 million incidents of intimate partner violence[16] (IPV) occur each year.[17] Even this startlingly high number likely is an underestimate, because most incidents are not reported. This woman's story was consistent with the way that experts describe the problem of domestic violence. Psychologist Lenore Walker was one of the early pioneers in the field and established many of the frameworks still used to discuss IPV today.[18] In her 1979 book *The Battered Woman*, Walker coined the term battered woman syndrome (BWS) to describe the effects of intimate violence on women. Although later researchers have critiqued and refined Walker's theories, her articulation of the key concepts of the cycle theory of violence and learned helplessness remain powerful descriptors of IPV.[19]

The cycle theory purports that domestic violence does not occur at a single constant level of intensity, but instead is characterized by three stages in a repetitive cycle.[20] During the first, tension-building phase, there are "minor" or "mild" abusive incidents, such as pinching, slapping, and verbal abuse, where the woman acutely observes her abuser and tries to modify her behavior to keep him calm. Next, tension escalates and the woman experiences a severe battering incident at the hands of her abuser. Then the third, "honeymoon" phase occurs and is characterized by the batterer's remorse and loving promises that the battering is over.

The theory of learned helplessness supplements the cycle theory, offering an explanation for why a woman might stay in a violent relationship. Walker suggests that as the violence repeats itself, the women come to understand that they have no control over when and whether their partners will attack them. Although they lose the ability to predict whether anything that they do will help to pacify or please their partners, they nonetheless continue to experience joy and pleasure during the "good times" with their partners. Eventually, this combination can be emotionally paralyzing, and the women become convinced that there is nothing that they can do to escape their situation.[21]

Ample research shows that abused women often are trapped by more than this cycle of violence or their fear of severe physical beatings or death threats. Women sometimes stay with an abusive partner for social or economic reasons.[22] Children, communal property, and an abuser's intimate knowledge of the woman's daily routine — basic details like the woman's place of employment, the children's school, family member's homes and mutual friends — can restrict a woman's options for escape. Leaving her abuser often requires abandoning her current life, moving herself and her children into an unknown and uncertain future. Escape routes for battered women typically are further limited by their partners, who isolate them from friends and family, minimizing their sources of support, and often leading them to accept their abuse as "normal." Women may also be concerned with the social stigma attached to IPV survivors and with the possibility that family and friends will be unwilling to help them to disappear and escape their violent relationships. Finally, women may fear losing custody of their children if they leave. One woman told us:

> One of the requirements of Children's Services Bureau (CSB) was to get my life together. My ex-husband was the one who was going to be my knight in shining armor. He was the one who was going to be stable. He was a truck driver with a regular job and no police record. He was going to come and get everything together. I got my kids back, we moved in together, and it went good for a month and a half and then he stopped taking his medication and would self-medicate. He was manic-depressive. I was going to stop the relationship with him, but I was afraid CSB would say that I would lose my kids again.

This theoretical backdrop helped us to understand why the women with whom we spoke tended to tolerate their partners' abusive behavior. As we listened more closely to the stories told by the other women we interviewed, however, we were struck not simply by the common experience of violence but also by the differences, both subtle and grand, in the manner in which these women experienced their violent relationships. It seemed clear to us that, although violence marked almost all of these relationships, there was a broad spectrum in terms of the ways that the women experienced and responded to the violence.

Mothers Who Kill and the Spectrum of Violence in Intimate Relationships

The observation that not all battering relationships are the same is not meant to excuse domestic violence in any of its guises. No one should be intimidated or abused, whether verbally, physically or emotionally, in the context of a loving relationship. But one can be misled by the terminology around domestic violence, in which terms such as "battering" might lead one to attribute uniformity to the experience of being beaten by one's partner. In addition, the common vocabulary used to raise awareness of violence between intimates might lead one to assume that the experience of such violence assumes an equally central role in the lives of "battered women." One might, on the basis of labeling a woman a victim of domestic violence, make a host of other assumptions about the woman's life — that she is vulnerable and trapped, that she is isolated from others, that she is attributes enormous power to her batterer, and therefore is unable to escape the relationship.

Our interviews with mothers who had killed their children revealed such assumptions to be, at best, only partial truths. Instead, almost all of these women spoke of lives that were complicated by dreams and realities that extended well beyond romance. Indeed, as most of these women told their stories, their intimate relationships with men assumed relatively minor roles, and the fact that these relationships were marked by abuse and intimidation often was mentioned in passing, as scarcely worth noting.

We have struggled to distinguish between the stories the women shared with us and the way that we, owing to our relatively privileged positions, heard their stories. Often, it was difficult for us to imagine any woman accepting the treatment that these women experienced in their intimate relationships. Most of the women seemed to expect relatively little from their lovers, whether as partners or as fathers. And many seemed to regard the abuse that came their way as normal.

We had a common vocabulary. In telling their stories, many of these women identified their relationships as "abusive" and noted that they had not understood this until after participating in the prison's domestic violence support group. The support group gave them a set of terms they could use in describing their intimate relationships. And yet, it was evident from the way they described the daily fabric of their lives that they ascribed varying levels of importance to these relationships and to the fact of violence within them. The terms they used to describe their relationships often concealed as much as they revealed.

The remainder of this chapter is organized around four stories of love and intimacy in the lives of mothers who kill their children. We chose these stories because they are examples that help to illustrate the surprisingly broad spectrum of experiences and reactions to intimacy and abuse described by the women we interviewed. We begin with the stories that most resembled the classic domestic violence scenario depicted by the academic and popular understanding of abusive relationships, and we conclude with the story of a woman who essentially had no relationship with either of her children's fathers. In telling their stories, we attempt to shed light on the role of male intimates and intimacy in the lives of mothers who kill.

Nadine's Story: Not a Love Story?

Long before her husband killed her seven-year-old son, beating him brutally one afternoon, while Nadine was away at work, Nadine had been familiar with intimate violence. She had been beaten and raped by her own father; her relationship with the father of her second and third children was so violent that the state took her three children from their home and placed them in foster care. Nadine had to work with child protection officials in order to regain custody. When Nadine returned home from work the day her husband fatally abused her son, she encountered a nightmarish scene. Her son lay moribund, and her husband brutally tore the phone from the wall and threatened to kill her and the other children if she attempted to get help.

In spite of the years of abuse, culminating in this gruesome murder, when she described her relationship with her husband, Nadine's eyes shone. She recalled the details of how they met, their first date, and the night they first became intimate, in exquisite detail. She did not communicate with him during the first ten years of their mutual incarcerations. In the eleventh year, he wrote to her at Christmas, sending a card with pictures of her surviving children, who live with his parents. She memorized his message, which she recited to us: "I hope this breaks the ice. I want you to know that I still love you." She answered with a card that said, "The only thing I still love about you is that you gave me two beautiful kids." But her eyes told a different story.

Experts believe that our understanding of intimacy and our behavior as adults in intimate relationships derives, at least in part, from our experiences of intimacy as children.[23] Although it is always difficult to determine the precise cause of human behavior, it seems certain that Nadine's experiences of intimacy as a child had a profound impact on her sensibilities regarding relationships as an adult. Nadine's biological parents had a violent relationship, and her mother escaped the violence by finding a new partner and moving away.

As we saw in the last chapter, Nadine did not blame her mother for abandoning her. Instead, she applauded her mother for having escaped her abusive marriage, even though she left her children behind with their violent father. It seemed obvious to Nadine that one should prioritize one's connection to one's lover over the connection to one's children.

Consider also Nadine's description of her childhood relationship with her father as "not physically abusive but sexually abusive." Oddly, by her own description, she suffered a considerable amount of physical violence at his hands. For instance, she noted that "I thought it was normal to get my ass kicked by my father." She recalled feeling relieved when, after three and a half years of living with him, her father "dumped her and her brother in Florida" with their maternal grandfather:

> I was relieved at that point that that part of my life was over. I didn't have to worry about being in the wrong place at the wrong time. I came home from work and he was pissed because someone cut him off so he'd beat the hell out of me. It's what he knew. He had a leather belt with his name and two different pictures of dogs. It was a man with blue stones for a pipe and fire in the pipe. You could read his name in my back through the blood.

Nadine's description of being victimized simply for being "in the wrong place at the wrong time" is consistent with standard descriptions of domestic violence.[24] The effect of such random violence can be particularly profound because it comes at the hands of those whom one loves. The conflation of love and violence formed a legacy that has played out in almost all of Nadine's other intimate relationships.

Her first long-term relationship was with Rusty, the father of her second child. (As we discussed above, her first child was fathered by a married man, for whom she worked as a babysitter.) She lived with Rusty on and off for several years. Her description of their relationship had many of the hallmarks of battering relationships. Rusty was jealous and possessive of her and kept her isolated from friends and family. She did not have a car, had a small child and no job, and was dependent on him. "[He] only took me to the grocery store, the laundry mat, and his mom's," she said.

Within a year, Nadine was pregnant with her third child. "We had a 'normal family life,'" she said. Her descriptions of the normal life, however, are harrowing. Both Nadine and Rusty used drugs, at first recreationally, but eventually, they assumed a larger role in their lives: "He was drinking every day. And then [he starting using] harder drugs (hallucinogens and marijuana). He introduced me to these. . . . he would hit me and I'd hit back. He'd threaten to have my kids taken away if I reported the abuse."

Nadine determined to leave him at one point in their relationship, and she moved into low-income housing with her three children, who were four, two, and eighteen months. She said she was afraid for her safety there, however, so she asked Rusty to move in to "keep her safe." She recalls drinking very heavily in order to tolerate him. ("As much as three-fifths of hard liquor a day," she said.) Rusty started using crack cocaine and soon found that he needed more money to support his habit. He began stealing, and then offering others sexual access to Nadine in order to satisfy his drug debt.

Eventually, their fighting drew the attention of the police. Nadine related that the police notified Child Protective Services (CPS) about their drug use, violence, and about the "messy house," and the children were taken into protective custody and ultimately were placed in foster care with Rusty's sister and brother-in-law. Nadine and Rusty separated for good. "He wasn't nice to me," said Nadine. "I had had it my whole life."

To hear her tell the story, Nadine's next relationship was remarkably similar to her relationship with Rusty. Ironically, Nadine seemed to be unaware of these similarities. She met her husband, Mack, at the bar where she was working after she and Rusty had separated and she had lost custody of her children. Despite her job, Nadine said that "she was trying to avoid drug and alcohol scene. He was a regular. He knew I needed a place to live and offered me a room. No sex, just a place to stay."

According to Nadine, Mack had an injury that made it difficult for him to climb stairs. She was to stay upstairs, while he slept on the couch. Then, after three months, on a Friday night, she was "celebrating" and had a couple of beers with Mack. They returned home, and Mack proposed that they share the bed, with her on one side and him on the other. "That lasted for a month," she said, with a smile, before they became intimate.

She told the story of their building romance slowly, and while Nadine tended to describe her role as that of an innocent, succumbing to seduction, she clearly felt pleased with the way that she made Mack wait for her. "I've always thought of myself as okay, not beautiful, not a dog, okay. I've learned I'm attractive to some men and here (in prison) I found out I'm attractive to some women. That blew my mind," she said, flipping her hair.

Over the ensuing years, Nadine described slowly discovering things about Mack. She did not know that he smoked crack until she was arrested on a parole violation and tried without success to reach him. It turned out that he was smoking crack with some friends. Then there was his story about why he had a parole officer. He claimed that his fourth wife had falsely accused him of beating her up. Even today, Nadine believes Mack's claim that he was innocent and had not abused his other wives. Later, when they moved to Ohio, Nadine found multiple prescriptions in the house and realized that he was abusing pain killers. Then she found injection-drug paraphernalia in their house.

In Ohio they had two children together. Nadine found a paying job, while Mack stayed at home during the day, caring for her three children from her previous relationships, and for their two babies. Over the years, he became "more violent toward her." He was jealous and possessive of her, beating her for suspected infidelities and flirtations. Although Nadine insisted that Mack had never hit the children, she noted that he had "spanked" seven-year-old Josh for soiling himself. She also recalled that Josh had developed a habit of holding his breath when Mack screamed at the family and that Josh had passed out and hit his head during one such episode.

One of the most troubling aspects of Nadine's story was that it was clear to us that she continued to trust Mack. She accepted his assertion that he never beat his fourth wife, in spite of her personal experiences with him. She accepted his claim that he never beat Josh, in spite of the symptoms of distress that Josh manifested. Even in her description of his actions, as he held Nadine hostage, preventing her from seeking help while Josh lay dying, there is a tone of understanding: "I don't understand how he could let his anger get away from him," she said, shaking her head sadly.

Nadine did not describe the positive aspects in her daily life with Mack. She insists that she had decided to leave him, coincidentally the day before he killed Josh, and that she was simply waiting for her paycheck in order to be able to afford gas and food. But it is not clear that even she believed that story. Her plans for escape were nebulous; she did not say how she was planning to leave, where she intended to go, and how she planned to support her children. Nadine never mentioned any friends or family outside her primary relationship with Mack. She was as isolated with him as she had been with Rusty.

Nadine seemed to accept her isolation as normal. As she describes it, her life revolved around the men with whom she was romantically involved. The only friend she ever mentioned was from school, which she left at age fifteen. And she had no ongoing contact with her own family. Like her mother, her primary bond seemed to be with her romantic partner, and like her mother, she would sustain that bond, even if it meant risking her own well-being and that of her children.

Patty's Story

Like Nadine, Patty had a long-term relationship with a violent man — the one with whom she had lived for years, first in her mother's home, and then elsewhere, starting when she was thirteen years old. Her boyfriend, Frankie, hit her from the beginning of their relationship. Although Patty did not use the lingo of those who had attended the prison's domestic violence program, she understood that the violence she endured was problematic. Thinking back on the relationship, Patty said, "He loved me in his own way. Not healthy." And like Nadine, her own family did little to teach her that one should not tolerate being hit by anyone, including a lover. Not only did her mother permit Frankie to live in the house, even though she knew he was hitting Patty, but she continued to undermine Patty's efforts to break off the relationship with him by letting Frankie return to the house.

At age seventeen, pregnant with her third child, Patty was living with Frankie and his family. Although Frankie's father was around "ninety percent of the time" and protected her from him, she determined to leave Frankie. "I finally had the courage to leave," she said. Certainly, given her young age, and her precarious circumstances, one can see that determination as courageous. In addition, she felt that Frankie was "[n]ot a good daddy. I felt like a referee when he was around kids."

She did leave, moving back to her home state, where she lived with her family. After she had her baby, though, she was reunited with Frankie: "Frank had a job. Things were good. Then Frank had a car accident and was in the hospital for a long time and couldn't pay bills so I went back home to Mom. I split up with Frank. It was always violent." This brief description is noteworthy, in that within the same thought, Patty says both that things were "good" and that they were "always violent." It is clear that, for Patty, a relationship could be both violent and good.

After she left him this time, Patty met a new man, Bill, who she described as "a good man, a good provider, and a good father." She became pregnant, and they married. Frankie was "out of the picture." Although she described Bill as a stable man who was "great with the kids" and had a job working for the city, it was clear that Patty felt little of the passion for him that she had for Frankie: "He didn't want to go out. He didn't like to spend a lot of time with me. I was drinking, smoking crack. I'd be with the kids [during the day], then [I would] party at night."

Her lifestyle took a toll on her relationship with Bill, and eventually, they divorced. Bill found a new partner, who did not want him to see the daughter he had had with Patty. Patty was despondent, and her drug and alcohol abuse increased. She attempted suicide by driving into a telephone pole, and while in the hospital recovering she determined that she "wanted to live for the kids." When she got out, she went back to her mother's and back to Frankie. Then she and Frankie moved out with the four children.

At first, she managed to stay away from drugs and alcohol, but there were financial problems; she found herself borrowing money and then selling and buying drugs to pay her debts. Gradually, she started drinking again. At first, it was only at home, in part because Frankie was possessive of her and would not let her go out. She stayed alone with the kids in those days, "and he's hitting me and spanking [them] for discipline."

She felt isolated in the apartment, with a violent, jealous spouse and four children. She met a friend, a man to whom her husband sold wood to heat his house, and she ran away to his house. There, she contacted Bill, who had separated from his new partner. Bill came and brought Patty and the four children home with him. By this time, Vicky, her daughter with Bill, was three. She and Bill reunited for six months, and Frankie was once again out of her life. But then Patty resumed drinking. She and Bill separated, and Patty moved into a rental home, supporting herself and her children on public assistance. She was again "drinking, but not drugging," she said, "and only after the kids were in bed." Her brother moved in with her, so that they could afford electricity and heat. Shortly after this separation, on a night when she was partying with a new acquaintance, her neighbor Rick (who currently is incarcerated for sexually assaulting a young girl), Patty's four-year-old daughter disappeared. Her body was found several days later, and Patty was convicted of having murdered her.

In some ways, Patty's "love" story mirrors Nadine's. Both were drawn to violent men, whom they tolerated in spite of the fact that these men provided them with very little support. Neither man was a trustworthy caretaker for their children; neither brought income into the household; both were emotionally unpredictable and abusive not only toward them, but also toward their children.

But Patty tells her story in a completely different manner than did Nadine. She does not see herself as having been a victim, without options, trapped in a cycle of abuse. Instead, she tells the story of a life in which she made choices, within a limited universe of options. Unlike Nadine, Patty was not isolated with Frankie but instead had a wide circle of family, friends, and "party buddies." She moved into and out of her relationship with Frankie numerous times over the course of ten years, exercising autonomy, in spite of having four young children, little education, no money, and no job. As she described it, Frankie was not the main cause of her troubles in life. He was simply a fixture, like her alcoholic mother. She blames herself, and her substance abuse, for the problems she has had. Although it is certainly possible to see Patty primarily as a victim of domestic violence, unable to break away from the man who tortures her, that version of her life is not one that she would endorse. Nor does it capture the small, yet extraordinarily resilient sense of dignity from which she draws her strength today.

Vanessa's Story

Although we spoke with her twice, and each interview lasted approximately two hours, Vanessa, who had raised her four younger siblings, and was living with her three children at the time of her crime, said little about the man who fathered her two youngest children. (Recall that her first child, born to her when she was fourteen, was fathered by a childhood acquaintance with whom she had no long-term relationship.) In telling her story, Vanessa spoke of her three children lovingly, calling them by name and describing the way she dressed and cared for them. Her partner, by contrast, she never named. She did not describe how they met or why they stayed together. Instead, Vanessa tended to speak of him in broad generalities, invoking the terminology that she learned in the prison's battered women's support group: "I was living in an abusive relationship, he was beating me, and sometimes the kids, too. I just kept it secret."

At the time of her crime, Vanessa was living in public housing and receiving public assistance. She likely would have had to conceal her partner's presence in her home, as access to these subsidies were predicated on her being able to establish financial need.[25] Although her partner was living with her and had fathered two of her three children, including the daughter who died, she noted that "he came and went as he pleased." Indeed, from her description of her daily life, it sounded as though he was gone from the home more often than not.

Vanessa said little about the nature of the violence that she experienced in her relationship. Her vague references to the subject suggest that the violence was intense. Yet, Vanessa's descriptions of her daily life include no mention of her partner. She had a broad network of family and seemed to be able to count on, and to be counted on by her cousins, aunts, and other relatives. She frequently babysat for large groups of children. And several times during the course of her interviews with us, Vanessa emphasized the fact that she felt independent and confident as a single mother: "I felt like I was independent. I was selling dope on the side. I had pride and was independent. Not thinking I wanted or needed help."

Vanessa credited the prison's psychiatric support program with helping her to identify domestic violence as a problem in her life. Until this intervention, she seems to have accepted her partner's abuse as unexceptional — what was to be expected from a man. One imagines that there must have been romance between them at some point; Vanessa is a proud, beautiful, and confident woman. But by the time she had three children under the age of five, her day-to-day life did not revolve around him. Instead, she was occupied with caring for her children, running her (illegal) business, and spending time with her extended family.

Marlene's Story

So prevalent was the fact of violence in the intimate relationships described by the women whom we interviewed that the few women who lived without domestic violence stood out as exceptions. Often, their secret to a life free from abuse was to forego relationships completely. Marlene's story is an example of this strategy.

Recall that Marlene describes herself as having been a terrible child, unable to focus, getting into trouble, and dependent on her mother's caretaking even when she became a mother herself. Marlene had her first child when she was nineteen and her second when she was twenty. Until her second child was born, she lived at home, with her mother, stepfather, and sister. After the birth of her second child, with the help of public assistance, she and her children moved into their own apartment.

Other than noting that her children had two different fathers, Marlene had little to say about the men in her life. She did not have long-term relationships with either man, and indeed, she did not refer to either of them by name in our two interviews with her. She struggled alone with the decision of whether to relinquish her second child for adoption. From her account, it seems that the baby's father was not at all involved in this decision, nor even necessarily aware that the baby was born. When we asked Marlene about her children's fathers, she said that the dads were "not around."

Marlene did not express regret over the absence of a husband or partner in her life. By her own account, she could have used another adult in the house to help her with the children and to help take care of the house.

Recall that in Marlene's case, the home in which she and her children lived was, even by her own admission, "filthy." She noted that, surely, part of the problem derived from the fact that she was "living on my own, on welfare, with no skills." She added: "Had I been normal, married with another person in the house — [a] husband — [that] might have helped. But I'm still me. I didn't have skills. If I would have been with my mother, she would've just done everything. It would've been fine." But Marlene was quite insistent that a husband or a partner wouldn't necessarily have saved her baby's life. She did not hold out hope for a romance that would have provided her with comfort, companionship, or even respite. Rather, the primary gain from having a husband, from her perspective, would have been to temper the harsh judgment of her community: "I was an unwed mother, two kids from different dads, on welfare. It was a stereotype. Had there been a clean house, husband, no welfare — different outcome. I wouldn't have been convicted."

Conclusion

At the risk of overstating the obvious, it seems important to note that the vast majority of women with whom we spoke did not have healthy, loving relationships with their partners.[26] Those whose partners remained involved in their lives after the birth of their children often were violent, typically both toward them and their children. They seldom provided support, whether financial or emotional. They were unpredictable. They were immature. And yet, at least for some of these women, these men represented their "least-worst" options.

In order to understand their choices in relationships, it is important to recognize the limited nature of the options that these women had. Overwhelmingly, they became mothers as teenagers — often as young teens. They did not finish school, they had few employable skills, and they had small children who needed to be cared for.

Many of these women lacked a safe place to live — or indeed, anyplace to live. For those women struggling to find housing, such as Nadine, their relationships provided them with access to a home with their boyfriend's parents. Life with their in-laws often proved to be almost as unstable and dangerous as life with their own families. In a surprising number of cases, the in-laws knew that their sons were abusing these women, but they did little or nothing to stop them. Moreover, many of the women reported that their in-laws were emotionally abusive, contributing to their sense of being trapped by their relationships.

As they told their stories about romance to us, it became clear that these women did not have a clear sense of how they would define a good, healthy relationship. Most of the women understood that abuse should not simply be the price that one pays for intimacy. But they offered no clear vision of what they wanted, needed, or expected in love. In describing her dreams for the future, Nancy, who survived years of abuse at the hands of her former boyfriend, Robert, said this: "I want a normal life: no abuse, to go to a beach, to get outside Columbus, to be a mom (not all alone). I need a partner, no abuse, and to go to Disney." In the minds of these women, a loving, abuse-free relationship was not a realistic dream; it was as elusive as Disneyland.

4

Mothering

Hopes, Expectations, and Realities

ONE SET OF questions that we knew we wanted to explore when talking with mothers who killed their children involved the differences between motherhood as they had anticipated it would be and motherhood as they found it to be. We expected to hear a lot about the gulf between the hope for cute, cuddly babies and the mundane reality of the daily, tasks of mothering. We did hear about that. What we did not anticipate, though, was the extent to which the experiences of these women in pregnancy and parenting would seem familiar, and even normal to us, in spite of the horror of their crimes.

Surprisingly, having killed one's child is not evidence that one was a bad mother. On the contrary, these mothers seem to have struggled to be good mothers and to have waged that struggle under exceedingly difficult circumstances. To be sure, the crime of filicide brands one as a failure at motherhood, and yet, these women reject that label, continuing to view and to value themselves as mothers.

In this chapter, we explore the journeys these women took into motherhood and what they found there. We begin with the circumstances of their pregnancies, which were marked by the familiar patterns of adolescent childbearing. Then we move on to consider the more extraordinary circumstances present in these women's lives — circumstances that shaped their experience of motherhood, and the extent to which they were able to succeed as mothers. Finally, we explore some of the common themes and lessons that emerge from these cases, as viewed by the mothers themselves, with the benefit, and the curse, of hindsight.

Unplanned Pregnancy and Unprepared Motherhood

One might spend decades reading about the problems associated with teenage pregnancy without ever getting at the core of what is truly troubling about it. Even the briefest of conversations with the women we interviewed helped to clarify the central ways that teenage pregnancy can be calamitous for the young mother. At least in this society, the problem with having babies as a teenager derives from the ways that adolescent mothers tend to be situated in terms of power and independence.[1] The women with whom we spoke were not merely young, but also relatively powerless when they became mothers. The majority had not finished secondary school; they had little means of supporting themselves and were dependent on the good will of others for housing, food, and support. Equally important, however, is the sense one gets that they were not emotionally prepared for motherhood.

Weighing the Options

When they became pregnant, all the women whom we interviewed had three basic options: keeping the pregnancy and becoming a mother; keeping the pregnancy and relinquishing the baby for adoption; terminating the pregnancy via legalized abortion. One of the more surprising consistencies to emerge from our interviews was the shared sense among these women that abortion simply was not an option. In spite of the fact that abortion was legal and that even the poorest of these women likely could have found ways to obtain the procedure, none of them considered terminating their pregnancies because they almost universally viewed abortion as morally objectionable. As one woman vehemently stated, "Abortion wasn't an option." Patty echoed this sentiment, even after becoming pregnant with her second child, when she was fifteen and had been taking birth control pills: "I never believed in abortion or adoption. It's mine. I'm taking care of it."

To some extent, one might view the failure to terminate their pregnancies as more than simply a moral stance. It also is a passive, as opposed to an active, choice. Obtaining an abortion would have required making a plan, gathering resources, getting organized, and taking action. Simply remaining pregnant did not require them to make any decisive changes in their lives. Vanessa's description of her response to her first pregnancy, at age fourteen, evinces some of this sensibility. She was afraid to let her parents, and especially her grandmother, know that she was pregnant: "She was a real church lady, my grandma." She tried to bring on a miscarriage by hurling herself from the monkey bars at school and getting into fights. But she did not consider an abortion, because she "didn't believe in it."

Laurie, who became pregnant when she was raped by her stepfather's best friend, did not tell anyone that she was pregnant. Her silence and inaction exemplify a passivity with regard to decision making about her pregnancy, as well as her deep conviction that abortion was wrong:

> I knew my Mom would understand because she was raped, but it would have been her and my stepdad. I felt ashamed and dirty, like I could have prevented this. He came over the next day like nothing happened. He told me not to worry about pregnancy; he had had a vasectomy. Then finally [he] came to the conclusion it was his. He told me he would set up an appointment in Columbus for an abortion. I didn't believe in abortion. I am religious and life starts at conception. I don't think anything rational clicked into my mind because I went on thinking day by day, not ahead.

Consider also the story of Nadine, who lived intermittently with her abusive father and her maternal grandfather. One day, when she was fifteen, her father and his then-girlfriend visited Nadine and her brother at their grandfather's home. Her father's girlfriend noticed that Nadine was pregnant. Without telling Nadine where they were going, the girlfriend and her father took Nadine to an abortion clinic. There, they learned that she was twenty-five weeks pregnant; too late for an abortion. "I did not want an abortion," said Nadine. "I had a plan of being the best Mommy in the world. Being there for everything. . . . I wanted to get education. . . . It didn't work out that way."

Nadine's father found a lawyer, and attempted to arrange for Nadine to relinquish her baby for adoption: "I feel he did not want to take care of my baby. I went and signed the papers but that was not what I wanted. . . . I didn't want her to grow up like me. . . . I had no means of support. No education. I would do this [relinquish her for adoption] for the best interests of the child." But when her baby was born, Nadine left the hospital without signing final custody papers. She brought her baby home to her grandfather's house and determined to raise her on her own.

One of the tragic consistencies among the stories told by the women we interviewed is that, although all of them ultimately chose to continue their pregnancies, and to reject adoption as an option, most did almost nothing to prepare themselves for the arrival of a new child.

Unplanned Motherhood

The contemporary culture of middle-class pregnancy anticipates that a pregnant woman will devote herself to planning for motherhood. A visit to the pregnancy section of the local bookstore will reveal shelves of books dedicated to the proposition that motherhood begins with pregnancy and that the way a woman behaves during pregnancy is directly connected to the welfare of her child-to-be. Pregnant women are expected to care for themselves with intense caution — obtaining routine prenatal care, refraining from alcohol, drugs, tobacco, caffeine, and avoiding a constantly changing list of foods thought to be detrimental to fetal development.

One of the more striking things about the pregnancy stories told by the women we interviewed is how little attention they paid to their pregnancies. They had few concrete expectations about motherhood. For the most part, they neglected to plan even the most fundamental things: where the baby would sleep, where they would live once their babies were born, how they would support themselves and their babies. To the extent that they thought about the future, they tended to think in the abstract, imagining their babies only as a source of attention and affection for them, rather than as independent beings who would place innumerable demands on them. Marlene acknowledged this wryly:

> Expectations about motherhood? Yes, when you are young and stupid, like I was, you don't look at the hard parts. Like it's going to be dependent on you for eighteen years. I knew that there was work involved from having had a little sister. But I wasn't thinking about being up all night. Just thought about how cute the baby would be and how people would tell me "how cute."

As they carried their pregnancies, their babies took on symbolic or instrumental value for these women. In a sense, the tendency to view one's babies in a symbolic manner is quite natural. Babies represent hope for the future, the potential for growth and change. For some of these women, the babies meant even more than that. They were the way that these women might secure not only attention and affection during pregnancy, but also a relationship and a place to live following the birth of the child.

Recall the manner in which Vanessa was able to use public assistance to support herself and her three children, thereby escaping the pressures she faced in her parents' home. Discussing this issue, she referred somewhat obliquely to the way that some girls use pregnancy to attempt to cement their relationships with men: "Some girls want boys to be a part of their lives. Do things for the wrong reasons."

It is evident that many of the women with whom we spoke were able to find places to live by virtue of having a baby. Some of them did this via public assistance, which became available to them as mothers of infants. Others found that once the birth of a grandchild became imminent, their boyfriends' families agreed to take them in. For example, pregnancy enabled Nadine to find a solution to the uncertainty surrounding her living situation, which revolved around her violent father, a grandfather who felt that she and her brother were too much for him to handle, and the constant threat of foster care. Once she had her baby, her boyfriend's mother permitted her to live with his family while she and her boyfriend tried to find a place of their own. Her baby thus helped to solidify Nadine's connection to others, tying her to a family and a home.

Motherhood and the Gap between Expectations and Reality

It is truly amazing how quickly a new mother comes to recognize the gap between the hopes and the realities of childrearing. With the first sleepless night, if not with the actual delivery of the baby, she recognizes that all prior expectations were somehow naive. The feeling of holding the baby may bring ecstatic joy, but after an hour of enduring its inconsolable crying, even the most confident new mother may question whether she will be up to the task of caring for this child. The shock must be even more intense for those who spend relatively little time preparing themselves for the transition.

A newborn has needs that are not readily confined to a fixed schedule, nor limited to specific hours in any given day. Unless she is supported by other caretakers who will attend to her needs, her household's needs, and her newborn's needs — a situation that was typical in premodern societies, but is far less common today in the West — caring for a newborn requires a woman to suspend her autonomy. A baby's needs are all consuming.

For the women with whom we spoke, the birth of their babies ushered in a time of chaos. Some of the chaos was fairly standard in nature, although that does not diminish its impact. Part of that chaos, though, stemmed from the fragile support systems that surrounded these women as they made the transition from girl to mother.

Destabilization: The Early Months of Motherhood

Much of what we heard from the women we interviewed about the early weeks and months of motherhood would have sounded familiar to anyone who has experienced the move into motherhood in contemporary Western culture. The hours are long, the baby cries, the mother occasionally feels lonely and isolated, wishing that her life would return to normal. "After I had the baby," said Nadine, who was then fifteen and living at her boyfriend's mother's home, "I had no money, and I was isolated. This was the biggest surprise about motherhood — that there were no other women around to help me." The feeling of isolation and the longing for a "normal life" did not necessarily dissipate with time.

The longing for a "normal life" is not unfamiliar after the birth of a child. Even women who spend years planning and hoping for a baby may long, once their baby is born, for a return to a routine that permits them a chance to shower, brush their teeth, and have a conversation with another adult. In the case of these women, however, that longing was intensified by the physical and emotional disruption that accompanied the births of their children.

Physical Disruption

Although some women found that having a baby helped them to secure a place to live, a surprising number of the women we interviewed were quite literally destabilized in the days and weeks immediately after giving birth — they lost their homes. They told their stories as if their struggle to avoid homelessness, accompanied by their newborns, was not particularly remarkable. They simply endured the uncertainty, taking with them their babies and whatever belongings they could carry. But the emotional and physical consequences of such instability take an enormous toll. Even in the least developed nations around the world, new mothers and their babies tend to be recognized as vulnerable and in need of support.[2] By contrast, these women's families were unable or unwilling to provide such support, and so, rather than feeling accepted and safe, these women and their babies often felt marginalized and desperate.

Consider Nadine's story. She had counted on living with her boyfriend, at his mother's home, after she had her baby. Her boyfriend's mother did not view this solution as permanent, however, and she told them that they could live with her for a few weeks, while they looked for housing and work. They found a place in a trailer park, but shortly after they moved in, her boyfriend began beating her and abusing drugs and alcohol. Without income or a means of transportation, Nadine's jealous boyfriend was able to isolate her, and with the exception of occasional visits to his mother, Nadine was cut off from any outside contact: "I had no understanding of why she [his mom] was so closed mouth. She must have been afraid she'd have to raise [my child] too. The only thing I did not have was female friends to ask 'Is this normal?'"

Like Nadine, Patty found herself moving with her infant children. Patty had been living with her alcoholic mother, her younger siblings, and her abusive boyfriend since she was thirteen years old. She told her story in a matter-of-fact manner, as if there was nothing particularly unusual or difficult about the instability she experienced between the ages of fourteen and seventeen, during which time she had three children. She described so many moves that, even though she was completely forthcoming about them, it was hard to follow her trajectory. Whenever we interrupted her to clarify, she calmly relocated us in the context of her life story, as she moved from one state to another, in any one of a variety of homes.

One woman told us of how her husband joined a traveling carnival where they were constantly "on the move — every week a new place." After she left her husband she strove to provide her children with a stable home. She said, "I wanted to give them a normal life after the carnival. So, I would have to say the majority of my time was spent trying to figure out how to get them a normal life — what society expected. Normal was having a home — a place to call yours — a family. That was normal to me."

Emotional Disruption

If one listens carefully to these stories, beneath the physical chaos of moving lies the emotional chaos of feeling unsafe. Even when they had housing, these young mothers knew that their "home" was unstable. They typically felt indebted to people whom they could not necessarily trust to protect them. The stories in which the young couple and their baby lived with the boy's parents are particularly telling. Although the gesture of providing housing to one's adult child and grandchild surely is generous, the young mothers we interviewed often did not feel supported by their in-laws. Instead, they seemed to live in their boyfriends' families' homes on sufferance, dependant on the continued good will of those who viewed them as burdens. Their emotional sustenance was derived from their children, who were, at the same time, the cause of their continued dependence upon others.

Nancy's story is emblematic of this problem. Recall that she had struggled throughout her life with the sense of being unwelcome and unsafe in the home that her mother had forged with her stepfather and her four half siblings. Almost a year after the birth of her first child, Nancy seemed poised to escape the violence she experienced at home by moving into her boyfriend's mother's home. Once there, however, she was met by another version of emotional and physical abuse. Although she claimed, in talking with us, that this living situation was acceptable to her, it is clear from her description that it was fraught with tension: "I felt in prison in his house. No one cared. My child and I were stuck in the house. He [my boyfriend] would say, 'Who else you gonna find who will take care of you?' He would taunt me in his own house saying, 'I have a high school diploma and you don't.'"

When she was pregnant with her second child, the tension became too much. Her boyfriend beat her in a fight triggered by his desire to get to a party. She and her son went to live with her father, who sexually abused her. She went back to live with her mother and lost everything in the move. Two or three weeks later, her daughter was born. Days later, she and her mother fought, and her mother threw Nancy and her children out of the house.

There was little or nothing in our experiences as mothers that permitted us to visualize with any presumptive accuracy the lives these women described having led as young mothers. It was emotionally exhausting to listen to their stories. Chaos permeated their lives; the mere description left us longing for quiet. Perhaps it is because of the constant noise and disruption in the stories these women told that we were not entirely surprised by their horrific endings. Nancy's crime, for instance, came at the end of eight weeks of moving from place to place, as she struggled to find a stable home for herself, her toddler, and her newborn. The story is tragic, to be sure, but in the sense of Greek tragedy — as if it had been foreordained and somehow called forth by all the forces of Nancy's universe:

I was back at Mom's the day I caught my case. I was hallucinating. She [the baby] wouldn't stop screaming, my son was screaming. I was trying to change the baby's diapers. I saw, in my mind's eye, my mom and sisters screaming and pointing at me. I just wanted to keep her quiet. I didn't want to kill my child. I just tried to keep her quiet. I covered her head and walked away. I just wanted there to be quiet. But I love my child just like I love my other children. I live with it every day.

Motherhood's Varying Norms

For all that was familiar in the mothering stories we heard, there were many ways in which these women's stories left us with the sense that we had entered a parallel universe to our own, one in which norms taken for granted in our daily lives simply did not exist. Nowhere was this feeling more powerful than in our conversations about the work of mothering and the expectations that one associates with being a "good mother." As is evident from the contemporary debates over day care versus maternal employment, even relatively affluent, well-educated North American mothers do not share a single definition of what it means to be a "good mother." Indeed, any discussion about mothering "best practices" is likely to generate disagreement, as well as defensiveness, even among seemingly secure, similarly situated mothers. This defensiveness bespeaks a level of insecurity. It may be that relatively few mothers of young children feel completely confident about their performance as mothers.

Our discussions about mothering with these incarcerated mothers were all the more striking in view of the uncertainty surrounding the definition of "good mother." Much of what these women unselfconsciously described as their mothering routine was out of keeping with the norms commonly articulated, if not embraced, by those who enjoy positions of greater power and privilege. It quickly became apparent that these women operated within a different value context when it came to raising their children. This is not to say that their standards for "good mothering" were necessarily lower than those professed by affluent women; indeed, the tasks that accompanied mothering for them often far exceeded what is expected of more privileged mothers.[3]

Defining "Normal"

As we have seen, these women spent relatively little time preparing for motherhood. They aspired to be "good mothers" and to have "normal family lives," but these words had nebulous meanings. For instance, consider Nadine, whose mother abandoned her, leaving her to be raised by a violent, abusive father. She recalls wanting to be "the best mommy in the whole world." She describes her life with Rusty, the father of her two children, in these words: "It was hard not to use drugs. We were just partying. We were evicted from low-income housing after Josh was born. We had a *normal family life* [italics added]. We thought we had it. Police get there [when called by the neighbors after a particularly violent fight] and he's telling officers that I beat him up. They asked, 'How big is this woman?' He punched me and I punched him back."

Recall Vanessa's struggle, from the time she was ten, to hide her parents' substance abuse and the chaos of her family's life from the outside world. When she became a mother, Vanessa redoubled her efforts to find stability. She spoke often in our time together of her preoccupation with "[t]he need to always 'make it normal; to keep it so that things seemed normal.'" To Vanessa, this meant that you "don't complain or call attention to problems." As a mother, she says, she was so invested in things seeming normal that she did not notice problems with her kids. In explaining why she chose not to seek medical treatment after her child was severely scalded when her older sibling gave her a bath, she said: "Kids will be kids. How do you determine whether it is serious? They [the prosecutors in her murder trial] say, 'She had to be in excruciating pain,' but she wasn't so I didn't seek medical treatment. If it is not bothering the kid it is not bothering me."

It is difficult to know precisely what these women meant when they spoke of "normal." Perhaps they meant unremarkable — nothing that those around them would deem extraordinary, and certainly nothing that would qualify as atypical or substandard in comparison to their own childhoods. Vanessa revealed this yearning for normalcy when she said, "My family wasn't abused. Got our ass whipped but wasn't poor, beat down, or taken advantage of."

To a large extent, it is the things that we experience when we are children that determine our baseline expectations for our own families as adults. We might aspire to do things differently, or better, but ultimately we all are in a dialogue with our pasts, as well as with our peers. In this way, one's own mother, one's childhood, and one's community work together to inform one's own sense of how to be a "good mother." It is a collective, rather than an individual sensibility that gives rise to motherhood's norms and expectations.

This insight is particularly significant in considering the stories of mothers who kill, at least insofar as they involve mothers whose children were lost because of mistakes and accidents that grew directly out of their parenting style — a style whose norms and expectations were shaped by others. For instance, consider the caretaking responsibilities shouldered by many of these mothers. In most cases, they reported having been solely responsible for their children, without any predictable or reliable source of respite from a spouse or other family members. In Vanessa's case, this expectation likely contributed to her daughter's death.

On the weekend that her two-year-old daughter died, twenty-year-old Vanessa had been staying alone in her cousin's two-bedroom apartment, caring not only for her three children, but also for her cousin's two children. All five children were under the age of six. There were no other adults in the home; no one stopped by to help her, to keep her company, or to give her a break. At night, Vanessa stayed in her cousin's room and locked the five children in the other bedroom. When we asked who was there to help her out that weekend, she looked at us quizzically. "My cousin was in Atlanta," she said. The idea of spending a weekend caring for five young children in a small apartment was unremarkable to her: "Somebody needed a babysitter, they would call me."

Vanessa was awakened by the children's noise before dawn. She yelled at them to go back to sleep. When she awoke, several hours later, she found her two-year-old dead in the bed. There is conflicting testimony as to how she died. Vanessa holds herself responsible for her failure to take her baby to the doctor. It never occurred to her to feel that the blame might also extend to those who would leave five young children in the care of a single adult, let alone one who is only twenty years old, for an entire weekend.

One other area in which mothering norms clearly diverged from those embraced, or at least espoused, by mainstream Americans involved the issue of corporal punishment. Although some researchers have noted a correlation between socioeconomic status and corporal punishment, more recent research suggests that the relationship is more complex and the use of corporal punishment is prevalent in the United States.[4] In any case, the overwhelming majority of women we interviewed reported having been beaten as children, and many of them admitted to beating their children, as well. It was interesting to note the norms that surrounded such punishment.

Vanessa, for instance, was careful to note that she did not beat her children with the extension cord, as they were too small for such treatment. "I used a belt when I was whipping my children. The kids were too young to use the extension cord," she said. She noted that, when she was little, she was hit with either the switch or the extension cord, and that the latter was excruciatingly painful. In a particularly candid moment, she recalled that, at her murder trial, she was asked why she had not used "time-outs" rather than hitting her children. "I laughed," she said. "Time-outs don't work for all children." She rolled her eyes just a little to emphasize how ludicrous it would be to try to impose a time-out on a three-year-old, while caring for four other children in a two-bedroom apartment.

Children as Property and the Lack of Boundaries

Psychoanalysts, psychologists, and the full range of mental health experts long have theorized that the central drama of the relationship between mothers and their children tends to involve the need to separate, and the difficulty of separating.[5] Much of the contemporary literature on the problem of maternal separation adopts the perspective of the child, discussing the negative consequences for a child of a mother's attachment style.[6]

In listening to these women talk about their children, we were struck by the extent to which they seemed connected to them. The women tended, in their conversations, to refer to their children as if they were extensions of themselves — almost as if they were their property. It is doubtful that they were exceptional in this regard. Nor were they necessarily wrong, at least not in the eyes of the law. Indeed, the law long has regarded the parent-child relationship as being governed by natural law, which simultaneously confers on parents both affirmative obligations and also a kind of property interest in their children.[7] As Professor Odeanna Neal explains:

> Three major themes govern the parent-child relationship: first, that the parents have a fundamental right to their children and to authority over them; second, that the relationship does not derive from, but is prior to the state, and is "natural"; and finally, that the right to and the authority over children carries obligations to care for the children. American legal ideology concerning the nature of the parent-child relationship was imported from British common law, which was itself rooted in centuries-old ideas about the parent-child relationship. Intertwined with natural law notions were ideas that children were also

the property of their parents, and more specifically, the property of the father.[8]

The women we interviewed were so explicit in articulating their sense that they owned their children that it led us to wonder whether they were simply saying aloud what all mothers, to some extent, feel.

Marlene, who acknowledged that she simply was not ready to be a parent, owing to her attention-deficit disorder and to her desire to "just be a teenager," was nonetheless clear about her sense that her child was her property. Recall that, in our interviews with her, she never said her baby's name. She talked with relatively little affect about her child. For instance, when commenting on her internal struggle over whether to place her baby with adoptive parents, Marlene said this: "From the beginning I struggled because you just don't give away a kid. I met the prospective parents several times. Felt bad changing my mind. Now it seems selfish, like the baby was 'mine.'"

In some cases, the sense of children as property was implicit in the mother's remarks. Consider the recollections of one woman (who purposely killed her children):

> I believe my children were happy with me. I was emotionally close with them. I was there for them twenty-four hours a day. If we stayed in a motel, we slept in the same bed — they always had a hand touching me. I provided for them before me. . . . They always came first. . . . I loved them very much. Killing them was not out of hate. It was a suicide. I could never envision them without me. I could not accept that someone could raise them better than me.

Similarly, there is a proprietary sensibility in Nadine's description of her children's custody situation. Nadine first lost custody of her children after the state Child Protective Services found that she and her boyfriend's drug-ridden, violent home was unsafe for the children. The children went to live with her boyfriend's sister and her husband, who did not have children of their own.

Perhaps it is natural that Nadine would resent these foster parents, viewing them as interlopers. She expressed no remorse about taking them from that stable home and moving them out of state when, many months later, she met a new man and was able to provide housing for the children.

Several years later, when she was convicted for murder for having failed to protect her son from her partner's abuse, Nadine's other children were returned to these foster parents. Nadine was furious about the court's decision to place them there, as her own mother had sought custody. Although her mother had never met the children, Nadine wanted her children to stay with her mother. Nadine's anger about the court's placement decision seems to reflect her view that her children were her property — that she should have be able to decide where her children would live because they belonged to her.

As noted above, to the extent that these women regarded their children as their property, they were not unique. It does not mean that they did not love their children. Rather, these mothers used proprietary notions to demonstrate their love for their children. The most vivid image of this sort of love comes from Vanessa. At age twenty, living on her own with her three little girls, Vanessa discussed the fact that she supplemented her public assistance by selling crack cocaine. She said, "My kids were my personal doll babies. . . . I wanted to make sure they were the prettiest girls around. I sold dope because I wanted them to have extra. So that everyone wanted to be their friends."

Reflections on What Went Wrong

Toward the end of our interviews with them, we asked these mothers to reflect on how the tragedies of their children's deaths might have been prevented. The answers they gave us were consistent: virtually all of them said that, had they told someone else about their difficulties, their babies would not have died. Literally speaking, this answer was quite true. In most cases, had there been even one other adult in their lives to whom they could have turned for help, their children would not have died when and how they did.

But, at a deeper level, their answers were unsatisfying. Despite years behind bars, and all the time they surely had spent mentally rehearsing what went wrong in their lives, these women seemed unable to imagine a very different outcome. Almost all of their stories reveal that, long before they killed their children, their lives were unfolding in a progressively chaotic manner. They were destined for a collision — the only question was who or what would be harmed in the crash. As Vanessa said, "If I wouldn't have come [to prison] when I did, I would have eventually ended up here . . . , or it could've been worse . . . could've been me or him [her partner]."

Although her words sound harsh, it did not seem to us that Vanessa was saying that it really would have been worse had she or her partner been harmed rather than her daughter. In fact, she was the only woman we interviewed who reminded us, when we finished our questions, that we had not asked her how she felt about her children: "I love my girls. . . . My baby dolls . . . precious. I never got to be a mother. What would she look like? What would she be doing in school? If I had it to do all over I would have sought medical attention." What she seemed to be saying, instead, was that things were out of control in her life and that it was impossible for her to imagine how harm could have been avoided.

Other women expressed the same sentiment. One woman said, "God doesn't want me to go through that. He took my son as a wake-up call." Another said, "Being here saved myself. If I had been out there, I'd be dead. I was on a suicide mission since I was 13." And finally, "I give God thanks every day. If not for God I would never have made it through all the things I have been through like an abusive relationship. I've seen death before my eyes so many times. If I hadn't come to the 'pen,' I might not be alive."

Maternal Isolation and the Risk of Harm to Children

On the narrow subject of avoiding their children's deaths, many of these women identified their isolation from other adults as a key contributing factor. Their families were not reliable sources of support for them; in the worst cases, they were quite the opposite.

As is common in relationships marked by interpersonal violence, many of the women whose partners beat them felt isolated and trapped in their homes. Nadine spoke poignantly of this isolation when describing her life with the father of her first three children, in which his fierce jealousy kept her alone, first in a trailer and then in public housing. The same was true in the case of the man who ultimately killed her son. She described a rage that led him to beat up the paperboy, as well as Nadine, after he caught them talking to one another.

Isolation in these women's lives, however, was not always literal. Sometimes, the women were isolated and alone, even though they lived with their families. For instance, Laurie concealed her pregnancy from her mother and stepfather, with whom she lived, because she was terrified about the consequences that would be set in motion were she to disclose it. In retrospect, she noted the obvious point that the best way to have prevented her baby's death would have been "telling someone."

Laurie's description of her daily life, during the months of her pregnancy, in a home she shared with her parents and her other children, helps to explain why she felt unable to disclose her secret. Rather than tell her parents that their friend had raped her, and that she was pregnant, Laurie said nothing. To the attentive eye, pregnancy sets in motion all sorts of changes, both physical and emotional. Laurie is a small, fragile-looking woman; the signs of pregnancy would have been unmistakable in her. Laurie experienced these changes alone, but her isolation was not simply self-imposed. Instead, her family helped to ignore her pregnancy. No one realized that her belly had become large and hard, as it does during pregnancy. Laurie said that no one noticed her belly because no one ever touched or hugged her; she felt, she told us, "invisible to them."

Vanessa's life, as a single parent of three children in public housing, reflected yet another sort of isolation. Vanessa saw her home as a refuge from her family and their complex, cumbersome needs and problems. Living on her own, with her three young children, she felt proud and independent. But the peace she bought came at a high price. There was no respite built into her daily life — just hours and hours with her little children. Even the most ardent middle-class "stay-at-home" mothers do not really stay at home in this way. They enroll their six-month-olds in "classes," or they arrange play dates for their one-year-olds, or they go to the park, even on the coldest days. One might claim that these activities are undertaken for the good of the babies, but the truth surely is more complicated than that. The mothers need to connect with other adults; they need companionship and distraction; they need ways to lend structure to their days.

Vanessa had occasional visitors; her children's father would stop by from time to time, sometimes acting violently toward her and the children, sometimes acting lovingly. Vanessa was dealing drugs, and she likely had customers who came to visit. But from the way that she tells her story, it seems evident that no one came to visit in order to help Vanessa with her children, or in order to give her a break from caretaking. She defined the job of mother as all encompassing, and it is hard to blame her for aspiring to that elusive, yet ubiquitous ideal. There is shame in asking for help: "The way I was with my kids, and other kids as well, nobody ever talked to me. My pride played a big part too. . . ."

The problem with predicating a prevention strategy on the narrow solution of "telling someone" or "asking someone for help" is that it is virtually certain that others already knew of these women's desperate circumstances. In many cases, those whom they would have told, such as their mothers, not only knew about their circumstances, but in large part had contributed to them. Consider Marlene's mother or Nancy's mother. What could these women have told their mothers that would have set in motion some progress toward stability and safety?

Maternal Responsibility

At the core of the stories told to us by the mothers who killed their children lies a heavy truth: these mothers were not that different from any other mothers we know. In the course of any given day, they had good moments as mothers. Sometimes, those good moments came when they were alone and at peace with their children. With measured eloquence, Nancy described one particular evening, in which she and her two babies had her mother's home to themselves: "I put my favorite song on repeat. It was "I Guess That's Why They Call It the Blues," by Elton John. I held my newborn in one arm, and my baby boy in the other, and we danced and danced until they got so sleepy and heavy that my arms almost broke. I laid them down on the couch, and then I lay down with them."

Perhaps the problem facing these mothers was not so much maternal isolation as maternal responsibility. They were fully and solely accountable for their children; there was no one else who felt that burden, no one else who was willing to help them shoulder it. As any mother, or indeed, as anyone knows, it is hard to string together one good moment after another. Inevitably, bad moments intervene. When those bad moments are horrific, as they were in these women's lives, we tend to let them eclipse any good moments.

In reflecting on these women and their stories of motherhood, it seems evident that there were both good moments and bad ones. Thinking seriously about preventing future cases of filicide requires that we acknowledge them both, rather than regarding these mothers as monsters. These mothers and their children had few of the resources they needed to build stable lives. The absence of resources is, at least in part, what distinguishes them from other mothers. Even with the luxury of hindsight, it is difficult to identify meaningful opportunities they might have had for ameliorating their circumstances.

As seen from the perspective of these women, it seems a distortion of reality to cast these tragedies solely as stories about mothers who failed. The truth is more complicated. These women embarked on motherhood early, and without sound support; they undertook the tasks of parenting largely alone, without reliable financial and emotional support from partners or families. Neither they, nor their families or communities viewed them as exceptional in that regard. These women, like other mothers, viewed their children with hope and saw in them the prospect of a better future. In some moments, they lived that future with their babies. And in other moments, that happy future proved to be elusive.

So great is the horror of their acts in killing their children that we tend to view them as non-mothers. We reduce the days, months, and years of mothering to the fact that they killed their children. Their transgression comes to speak for the entirety of our sense of them as mothers. Without a doubt, though, to the extent that we wish to understand these women and their crimes, we must listen to the rest of their mothering stories.

5

Punishment, Shame, and Guilt

IN THE COURSE of the telling of their stories, the women we interviewed spoke with great candor about their lives behind bars. Time and again, they alluded to their feelings of guilt and shame, and to their struggles to come to terms with what they had wrought. Ironically, though, their experience of incarceration itself was not necessarily negative. Indeed, for many of these women, incarceration was a surprisingly positive experience. This is not to say that they felt that they had escaped punishment, but rather, that punishment for these women did not take the form that one might have expected.

When it came to speaking about incarceration and its meaning and effect on their lives, the stories told by the women we interviewed often varied depending on how long they had spent behind bars. More than one-third of the women discussed how, over time, incarceration had led them on a personal spiritual journey. The early stages of the journey were marked by anger and denial, self-loathing, and shame. Those who moved through this phase embarked on efforts at reconciliation, typically by reaching out for help from others. Finally, there were some who, after long years of work, arrived at self-acceptance and forgiveness.[1]

The Early Years

It is not surprising that many of the mothers we interviewed were full of anger and denial when they first arrived at the women's reformatory. Denial is common among prisoners, and indeed, because we are living in an era in which the problem of wrongful convictions has received national attention, we were keenly aware that at least some of the protestations of innocence we heard might have been legitimate.

A second, more common version of denial among the women we interviewed involved claims that they were not blameworthy because they had not committed an affirmative act, but rather, had done "nothing," or had simply made a mistake. For instance, one of the women (who had left her children unattended then a fire broke out) maintained:

> It was faulty wiring . . . she died from smoke inhalation. That word kill . . . I didn't even hear that in court. Some women aren't where I'm at and hearing that word might even traumatize them . . . harsh word . . . I didn't line my kids up on a couch and shoot them . . . I read *Jet* magazine and a lady let a baby go outside and a dog ate the baby up and [it] wasn't the first time and they charged her with child endangerment misdemeanor. Maybe the lawyer should have fought for me. I got child endangerment because kids were in the house and I wasn't. I pled no contest to involuntary and child endangerment. Ended up paying the attorney . . . I am angry at him. . . . Had a good judge but I was used as an example. The judge said, "You made a mistake." I don't think people should be punished for a mistake.

To the extent that the women were occupied by feelings of anger and denial, they tended to act out violently. Many of the women with whom we spoke recalled acting out in the early months of their incarceration and being forced to spend time in "the hole," or solitary confinement. For instance, one woman recalled: "My initial way of dealing was with crying, anger, fighting. . . . I just wanted to hurt people they way I had been hurt. . . . I tried to commit suicide — pills, lashed out, stayed in the hole. . . . I realized that I was the only one hurting me. So, I had to change my attitude. Now staff compliment me that I calmed down and that makes me feel really good."

Many women were suicidal following their crimes. Indeed, many had attempted, without success, to kill themselves along with their children. On admission to prison, they often persevered in their desire to die. For instance, one woman reflects back on her powerful wish for death:

> My next chilling thought was that I want to die and I want the kids with me in death. . . . Feelings resurfaced that I wanted to die. Everything I valued was my kids and if I had them with me in death then there was nothing holding me back. . . . [When I met my lawyers] I told them flat out that I would accept the death penalty. I wanted that avenue to be sure that I could die.

As the feelings of anger subsided, they often were displaced by feelings of self-loathing, a torment induced by reliving, over and over, their children's deaths. The women's faces became distorted with pain as they described the weight of the memories that they carry with them. More often than not, words failed them, and they began to cry as they described the pain of living with the knowledge that they had killed their children. Here are several different women's expressions of this pain:

> You know it's easy to sit back now and say I should have done this, I should have told him I'd leave. The worst case scenario at that time would not have been as bad as what happened. In November . . . it was the anniversary of my son's death and um . . . [she cries and takes a long pause]. I don't know, it just never gets easier. I used to go into a big depression for two or three months at that time of year. I was thinking the other day about how old he would be and when I look at my son I feel such guilt over that fact that he was never allowed to grow up.

> Not a day goes by I don't think of my son. Because you're guilty of something — you did it. There's nothing a court can do to me that I can't do to myself. What kind of mother am I? I went through Tapestry [a support group for incarcerated women] and it was the only thing I couldn't talk about.

> Sometimes I think that the closer you get to God, the more the devil tries to pull you away. . . . I haven't really gotten over the anger about my daughters . . . it is so hard for me to accept that my daughter is gone. The lawyer sent me all these pictures of the fire . . . and my daughter . . . it didn't look like her. I decided to get rid of them and the chaplain and I looked at them together and burned them up. The fire investigator thinks that if I hadn't left her unattended, that it wouldn't have been a fatal fire. . . . I used to read that stuff over and over again and it makes me feel pretty guilty.

At the end of the second of our interviews with Vanessa, we felt as though we had covered every angle of her story. We had talked about her children, her daughter's death, her childhood, her partner, her time in prison. There had been time for tears and time for anger. We asked her, as we did all of the women with whom we spoke, if there was anything she wanted to add; she said, "You didn't ask me how I felt about my daughter."

It became clear to us, as she answered, that words could not begin to convey the depth of emotional pain that marked her daily life. She said:

> A day doesn't go by that I don't think about my daughter [she cries and pauses]. You learn from mistakes and pay for mistakes. If other kids hadn't been in the house . . . Took me a minute to realize something was wrong. You don't think something like that will happen in your household. I wasn't me, wasn't myself. . . . What was she thinking? Was she wanting me? Trying to call me? She just looked peaceful. . . . She was "dead on arrival."

Stigma and Scorn

One of the common themes reported by these women was their sense of public humiliation and shame. Many felt judged, and to some extent misjudged, by society at large, as well as by their fellow inmates. As one woman reflected: "The system has treated me well. . . . I can't say that for the inmates I live with. They are judgmental when they don't know me and hear about my crime. Most of my fellow residents are nice but if they are in here for, like, forging checks, they think, like, 'My crime's better than yours.'"

It is evident from the interviews we conducted that there is a perceived hierarchy of crimes among incarcerated women, and that in that hierarchy, killing one's child ranks decidedly low. As such, the women with whom we spoke were reluctant to discuss their crime with others and often were shamed by other inmates when they learned of their actions:

> A lot of people here call me "baby killer" and it bothers me. People say I'm a violent killer. It's not that I purposefully did anything to them. . . . I am not a violent person. When they call me baby killer, it is really painful. I don't think I killed my children. . . . It is hard to deal with . . . being in here . . . hard to understand how my family can stick by me . . . because I have a lot of guilt and I started hating myself and I am thinking, how can they not hate me?

Many of the women with whom we spoke had internalized this sense of shame. They avoided talking about their crime with others, and, to the extent possible, kept secret the reason for their incarceration. Many of the women told us that our interviews marked the first time they had discussed the events surrounding their children's deaths. One woman, who had been insightful and forthcoming in our first set of interviews, declined to participate in the second set of interviews. "I poured my heart out that time, and there's nothing left. I can't go back there again," she said.

But it was clear that the women do "go back there," at least in their own minds, time and again, and that acknowledging their mistakes and contending with their shame seems to play a central role in coming to terms with the magnitude of their losses. For instance, we spoke with one woman in our first set of interviews whose children died in a fire started while they were left home alone. When we asked her how she coped in her daily life, she said:

> Because I try to recognize what it is about me that makes me feel guilty and accept those things. I'm looking at it in a different point of view, rather than "I'm stupid and irresponsible." . . . I can't bring my kids back by being guilty and shameful. . . . It's hard because sometimes I wake up and I don't want to get up out of bed and I feel horrible. . . . I don't want that for myself. I don't feel I deserve it. I know I didn't deliberately do anything wrong . . . that I made a bad mistake . . . no one else lost what I lost . . . just because I'm not unhappy all the time doesn't mean that I don't miss them. But I have to keep going on living.

Others acknowledge the horror of their crimes but object to the perception that those who kill their children are necessarily worse human beings than are those who commit other crimes. Indeed, one woman reflected on her struggle to get her fellow inmates to understand her crime in the context of the turbulent environment in which she had been attempting to raise her children:

> Everybody looks at child crime as the worst there is, but they need to look at individuals. . . . They let girls here for drugs out — why can't we get out and get help? They will keep doing drugs and come back here, but women who kill their children never come back. We need help. One of my stipulations should be that I get counseling. . . . A girl here made a comment that "I wouldn't want you as my neighbor." Women

who kill their children have less than one percent chance of doing it again. People have to stop . . . thinking that we are cruel and hard; we just went through an emotional battle. I've had girls tell me that they went through what I went through but they had their husbands and mothers to help them through it.

Rationalization and Reconciliation: Finding a Context for Processing Guilt

Guilt is a paralyzing emotion. The women with whom we spoke, and in particular, those who had served at least several years in prison, coped with their guilt and shame by taking affirmative steps toward recovery. These steps tended to take one of three courses. The first, and most commonly mentioned step, was the help they obtained from prison psychiatric services. The second road to recovery, or at least to acceptance, lay in religion. And the third mechanism by which these women learned to cope was by forging alliances with other women, to whom they came to refer as their "prison families." These three survival mechanisms are by no means mutually exclusive, but the women tended to view themselves as drawing their strength from one of these three sources.

Psychiatric Services

The Ohio Reformatory for Women's (ORW) office of mental health services was not a particularly well-financed ward. Situated in an old office building on the prison campus, it featured small rooms with peeling paint on the walls. The metal, wall-mounted radiators sporadically gave off steam heat, regardless of the outdoor temperature, and the barred windows seldom could open. The doors on the bathrooms in the offices did not quite shut. Occasionally, guards' voices, shouting orders or just chatting, could be heard over the hum of overhead fluorescent lights and the constant noise of footsteps and voices of people passing in the halls.

At any given time mental health services at the ORW has a staff of approximately forty-six. These include psychiatrists, psychologists, social workers, activity therapists, psychiatric nurses, and certified professional counselors. Prior to 1993, mental health services at the Ohio Department of Rehabilitation and Correction (ODRC) was understaffed and employees received very little training.[2] In 1993, however, two events occurred that affected the future of mental health services in the ODRC. First, there was a prison riot at the Southern Ohio Correctional Facility in Lucasville, in which nine inmates and one employee were killed. After this, the ODRC was placed under careful public scrutiny. In the same year a class-action suit was filed in federal court by prisoners with severe mental illness claiming mental health services within the ODRC were "deliberately indifferent" and deficient.[3] This litigation resulted in a five-year consent decree known as the Dunn Decree. The Dunn Decree allowed for numerous reforms, including increased staffing and increased education and training for inmates and staff.[4] The Dunn Decree terminated in 2000, and although the budget for mental health has decreased slightly since 2000,[5] staffing and training increases have been sustained.

In the years since the Dunn Decree period has ended, Ohio has been able to maintain its mental health system. Approximately 4 percent of the correctional budget is allocated to mental health services. This funding must meet the needs not only of those prisoners who are designated as mentally ill (approximately 16 percent), but also of those who, because of their behavior, or their self-identification as someone in need of services, are on the mental health services caseload at any given time. Typically, this latter figure represents up to 45 percent of the women incarcerated at ORW.[6]

In keeping with the current trend favoring the pharmaceutical treatment of mental health disorders, many of the women we interviewed referred to being "on medication." Some, like Nancy and Marlene, felt comforted by the diagnoses they received; the fact that they had a disease helped them to understand the reasons for many of their past struggles, and they accepted that they would need medication for the rest of their lives. Others rebelled against the medication, feeling that the medication made them dull and lethargic, rather than helping them. Still, none of the women we interviewed was being involuntarily medicated.

At first glance, "Psych Services," as the inmates call it, scarcely inspired confidence. We were surprised, then, to hear it praised by the women we interviewed. Nancy, for instance, credits the ward, its staff, and programs with keeping her alive: " 'Psych Services' is my second home. I love this place." The women reported finding solace in their relationships with their therapists, who helped them to understand their actions in the context of their entire lives, rather than simply as evidence of their failure as mothers. One woman describes the way she uses denial as a coping mechanism,

and how her therapist is helping her to recognize that tendency and to
begin to work through her grief:

> I mean a lot of it is, like I think, denial. Sometimes I am in denial that I
> am even in prison because it is not what I thought it would be like. I'm
> in denial that my children are gone. It is easy to pretend they're home.
> I'm coming out of that denial after working with [her therapist]. Just
> learning to work through things . . . to not shut out or block things
> out. . . . I mean, that is what I've done my entire life . . . there are large
> parts of my childhood that I blocked out. I know it's not healthy.

The women tended to describe their therapeutic relationships in terms
of the safety of the space that their therapists gave them. When one considers how little peace and safety these women knew in their lives outside
of prison, it is easy to see why, once they grew to trust their therapists,
they might cherish that connection. Consider this story from one of the
women with whom we spoke:

> I love myself, [am] at peace with myself. My daughter sees me every-
> day. Feelings that I get, no matter what — she is with me. At first I
> didn't have that. The therapist I had took me through changes. There
> are times I would come into here and just scream. I didn't talk to just
> anyone. But then [her therapist] made me dig all from my childhood
> to here. First step is acceptance and go from there. I keep a journal.
> I pray all the time. That's my serenity. My understanding about why
> things happen way they do. . . . Today — I love myself and I can do
> anything I put my mind too. I feel I'm untouchable. I refuse to re-
> gress and go back to the same old . . . "I don't give a shit" attitude. It
> doesn't get easier because it's an every day thing. It's just in the way
> you process it and deal with it. When she comes into mind it sits me
> down . . . it sits me down.

Religion

Among the women with whom we spoke, solace also was sought, and
often found, in religion. For many, there was some comfort found in belief in an all-powerful deity, who had ordained all of the events that had
come to pass in their lives. This sort of faith had the effect of relieving one
from ultimate responsibility for having killed one's child. Nancy reflected

this sensibility when, in the middle of her interview with us, she forlornly remarked, "Of all the things in my life, why did God choose for this to happen?"

Even the most ardently religious of the women we interviewed were not able to relieve their guilt completely by way of their conviction that a supreme being had caused their actions. For instance, one of the women we interviewed acknowledged her sense that belief in a deity provides an easy, if not always persuasive excuse for her actions. When she mentioned her faith, she noted that, at present, she was "not close to God":

> I think I should be because my children are with him and I'm the mother of two little angels in heaven, but I feel like God abandoned me when I needed him most. But then I realize God never abandons you. I do kinda believe that everybody has a time to go and maybe nothing could have changed it. Maybe there is a purpose to be here. Sometimes I think maybe it's the easy way out to think that, because everybody says that if I hadn't left them alone that they wouldn't have died.

Instead of looking to a deity to excuse one's actions, some of the women tended to view religion as a source of strength and love. For instance, the comments of one woman regarding her relationship with the divine are not terribly different from others' comments regarding psychiatric services:

> I've grown a lot. When I first got here, I was a nervous wreck. I worried about what people thought of me. I felt like I was alone. I know other people like me or are in worse situations. I could've been the one dead. I'm there for my children. Now I know the mistakes I made and I've reflected on my life. It's like a movie. . . . I play it over and over again. I know how I want it to be different. Back then, everybody I was hanging around, everything was negative. You realize who you can depend on is mainly family . . . the only person I really need now is God and I think this time I'm gonna make it.

One of the most interesting aspects of the women's discussions of their relationships with the divine lay in the way their faith lent a sense of mission to their lives behind bars. Several of the women we interviewed professed their faith that they were in prison for "a reason." Celina, whose child died from abuse at her own hands, said:

Since I've been here I've found Christ but I didn't know that before. . . . I want to know [Him] but . . . I was mad at Him for not helping. He [she cries] knew what I went through in my daddy's basement. I was mad at Him but now I know He had to take my daughter to save my soul. I know in my heart she's my guardian angel. Now today instead of people helping me, I help them. I am there for them. I know I'm saving souls today. God has done such wonderful things with me since I have been here, showing me He never left me. I know He's with me. I have friends here that have the same charges I have. Mine was an accident; why did I get seventeen years, why would He give me all this time? I know it's because He's got work for me to do here. . . . I know God put me here for a reason. I have to be with people. Now I am talking freely. Two or three years ago, I would try to hide things but now I can talk about how I am recovering.

Not only has Celina "found Christ" but she said her family is also being saved by her intervention. She stated: "[My mother] could never have known Jesus if not for me. I know he is living in her heart because of me. I am the reason most of my family is saved today."

It is not uncommon for those facing long prison terms to cope with their incarceration by way of faith. Indeed, even Enron founder Kenneth Lay, who died of a heart attack shortly before he was to be sentenced for fraud and conspiracy for his role in perpetrating the largest case of corporate fraud in U.S. history, was reported to be coping well with his pending incarceration because "he believed God may have had a purpose for him in prison."[7]

Religion is a mechanism for permitting one to conceive of oneself as being worthy of love. Over and over again, the women with whom we spoke testified to the manner in which their faith motivated their desire to make a difference for the better in others' lives. In addition to psychiatric services and religion, many women found not only solace, but a sense of purpose in the communities they built behind bars.

Community and the Prison Family

Many of the women we interviewed spoke with deep passion about their connections to other inmates. For instance, when asked to describe the effect of incarceration on her, Vanessa said: "Effect of incarceration? I got a family in here. At first, I was in denial and defensive. I'm a whole different person now. I'm family for people in here who don't have family. I still don't know what my purpose is, but I'm here to help people, not to judge them. My favorite quote is Matthew 7: 'Judge not lest you be judged.'"

In view of the fact that Vanessa describes herself as always having been a "caretaker," whether it was for her four younger siblings and her parents, or for her three babies, it is not surprising that she would seek solace in finding those who need her. It is important to notice, though, that her description of her family in prison is unlike her family outside of prison. She is "here to help people," but she does not need to take care of them at her own expense, as she did with her own family on the outside. Instead, the first thing that comes to her mind when she thinks about the effect of prison on her is to comment that she has built a family by allowing herself to be vulnerable — no longer "in denial and defensive." Such vulnerability was a luxury that Vanessa could not afford in her life outside of prison. It is easy to imagine the impediments to intimacy created by denial and defensiveness. This posture helps us to understand why she found herself in a situation in which she could not ask for help.

Likewise, Nancy, whose home life was marked by emotional exile and physical abuse, describes the comfort she derives from her friends in prison. When we asked her about the extent to which she saw herself as being different from other mothers, she answered: "I hear women here now wouldn't dream of doing that to a child. Some say that they did. Shook kids and never got caught for it. Some know I'm not a monster. I am a beautiful person. I love everybody."

When Nancy entered prison, she recalled, she felt completely loathsome. It is unlikely that she enjoyed many opportunities to feel like a beautiful person in the years of physical and sexual abuse she endured at the hands of her parents. Indeed, after she killed her daughter, but before she was arrested, her parents meted out their own punishment: "After I caught my case, my dad held me back and let my sister attack me." The empathy she received from those of her fellow inmates who confessed to having shaken their children came to her as a gift. In view of her past, to be accepted as other than "a monster," and validated as a "beautiful person," likely gave Nancy a sense of comfort that had, heretofore in her life, been missing.

One of the women with whom we spoke was particularly eloquent in describing the therapeutic effect that her prison friends have had on her recovery:

> Since I have been in here I worked on myself. When I came I was suicidal and I went on meds and also started doing programs, so this won't happen again and so if I think about it, it won't depress me and drive me back to being suicidal. . . . I feel more cared about in here even though I am in an institution. I have friends here that know what happened and care about me. I can't forget it. I get it bad when I see others' pictures of babies and commercials because I feel it was wrong to take another life but there's nothing I [can] do to change it. I think that this is the best thing that happened to me — to come here and get my life back together.
>
> There's a lot of nice people here and stuff. . . . I haven't seen the hole in four years. I have gone to cosmetology school and take my state boards in February. . . . I have done groups. I am in the gospel choir. I dance. I play volleyball. Basically, I have done all the groups I could. I am in Narcotics Anonymous. . . . I can't stay still because then, I just think. In a single room, I get to thinking. Other than all of that, I keep busy and a lot of ladies come to me to talk. They say stuff that I say means something. I like helping others.

"Prison Saved Me": Achieving Self-Acceptance Behind Bars

The deepest irony to emerge from the many hours that we spent talking with mothers who killed their children lay in the fact that so many of them described their years behind bars in such a positive manner. This is not to say that most of the women were not eager to be released. Indeed, many of them started their conversations with us by referencing their "out" date, or noting the timing of their next hearing with the parole board. Nonetheless, the majority of women with whom we spoke reflected the sense that prison had changed their lives for the better.

To some extent, this fact should not surprise us. The vast majority of these women endured lives marked by chaos and danger prior to their convictions. Often, their ability to meet even their basic needs was limited, and there was little they could take for granted in their daily lives as children, partners, or parents. As Abraham Maslow observed, until one's foundational needs for shelter, nourishment, and safety are met, higher-level needs such as love, esteem, and self-actualization remain elusive.[8]

By providing a predictable, structured, and relatively safe environment, prison stabilized the foundational needs of the women we interviewed. As a result, they were finally permitted to develop a deeper sense of meaning and purpose, and over the course of time, of self-acceptance and even of love. The process of coming to terms with one's self, particularly in view of the nature of their crimes, seems to be a slow one. For the most part, the women who most reflected the sense of having taken responsibility for their pasts, and having come to terms with their crimes, were those who had spent relatively longer amounts of time in prison. After nine years behind bars, Laurie's remarks conveyed this sense of growing self-respect and love:

> I've grown so much since I came here. I'm not the shy, timid person that I was. You could have walked all over me out there. But in here, I'm taking care of myself. At home, I wouldn't speak my mind, but in here, I speak my mind. It took me a bit to see, but in here you've got to stick up for yourself. . . . This is a real big wake up call, but this is also a lifesaver for me. A lifesaver because I got to know myself and am getting to know myself better each day. . . . In here, I make my own decisions and I'm my own person. I can finally look in the mirror and smile at myself. At home, I looked in the mirror and didn't think I was worthy. I didn't think I was pretty enough or good enough. . . . Now I can look at myself and say, "you're worthy of this." At home I felt lower than dirt.

As they came to accept the reality of their lives behind bars, some of the women began to find meaning, and even joy, in their daily lives. Feelings of happiness often triggered a sense of guilt in these women, though, as they felt that, because of their crimes, they were not entitled to feel happy. For instance, one woman, who had already served more than two decades for killing her children when we interviewed her in our first set of interviews, said:

> Before I committed the crime, I didn't like any of me anymore. I didn't feel I could be a good person for many years. I didn't accept I could have a life after killing my children. One of the people who became a

good friend of mine sat me down in the "rec" room and she had me focus on my feelings and what I did to my kids and what I did to myself. Once I started to be challenged to be introspective, I could admit and accept responsibility for that moment and every moment of my life. Once I reached a point where I felt responsible, I stopped having nightmares about my kids. I had good dreams — of us doing things together. They could be different ages. It was the spiritual image of who I thought they would become.

Conclusion

Not all the women became introspective and philosophical over the course of their years in prison. But those who succeeded in attaining a degree of self-acceptance and love had come to terms with their pasts and had devised a sense of mission and meaning that infused their daily lives with purpose. Consider the remarks from this woman, who had served many years in prison:

> Do something with your time — you've got to get back to the community in one way or another. It irritates me when women with cases like mine act nonchalant — that's because you're not dealing with it. Why you sitting here? Don't brush it under the rug! Why are you here . . . you need to think about why you are here. The bottom line is a child or children died. You need to sit down and think about why you are here. Pisses me off. When I get like that, people don't understand me and they shut down. Now that I voice how I feel, they shut down. I get on my bunky all the time. Everything is fine and nonchalant. You need to think about the fact that you broke your baby's arm and that's why you are here. Can't nobody make you happy but you. A lot of times I get so frustrated I just pray. I was like they are; I was afraid to say anything, it was a process. [I am] . . . coming out of my box and now I am completely out. That's why I feel really good about myself and I just think that anybody that has a case like mine needs to work A to Z. Nobody can do it but you and God. He knows where your heart is at and will make sure you get there but there'll be trials.

Another woman with whom we spoke had just heard from her surviving son, for the first time in over a decade, the night before our interview.

Although shaken, she remained composed as she told us: "It's at the end. There's no more. It's behind me, in the past. I take responsibility. I see things that I could have done, and that's going to have to be enough cause I can't do it over. It'll be all right."

PART 2

Making Sense of the Stories

The stories the women told us reflected their own sense of what mattered to them, what motivated them, and what went wrong. They were, by definition, individual and personal. Perhaps because their realities were so different from our own, we found ourselves searching for patterns in their stories, setting them against a backdrop that might afford us some insight into their actions and give us a better sense of how things could have turned out differently.

In these final chapters, we attempt to make visible the social, cultural, and class backdrop that informed the lives of the women with whom we spoke. Of course, in so doing, we have been informed, and perhaps misinformed, by a backdrop of our own — one marked by our own relative privilege and power.

6

Interactions with the State

Holes in the Safety Nets

IN LISTENING TO their stories, it often seemed that harm of some sort was bound to come, sooner or later, to the children of the women with whom we spoke. Trouble was a constant drumbeat in the background of their days, sometimes louder, sometimes quieter, but always present and always ominous. Most maddening is that, in retrospect, the terrible harm that did come to pass were both foreseeable and ultimately preventable.

These women were well acquainted with the safety net of public institutions designed to serve and to protect the vulnerable. Indeed, they practically were born into that safety net. They knew the safety net as children, as parents, as crime victims, and as criminal defendants. They seemed accustomed to living in the omnipotent gaze of various state institutions — social workers, welfare bureaucrats, housing officers, lawyers, probation officers, public health workers, school teachers, hospital personnel. But in the end, all systems failed to protect them, and their children, from harm.

The "safety net" is an apt metaphor: a net has gaping holes; it is composed of narrow ropes; it may well be easier to get ensnared in it than to be "saved" by it. At one level, this chapter explores the failure of the safety net in these women's lives. At another level, it tells a more complicated story. Often, one hears talk of the vulnerable being harmed after they "fell through the cracks" of the system that was designed to protect them. These women's stories illustrate a different, less passive dynamic. They and their families seldom *fell* through the cracks. Rather, they moved into and out of reach of the system, in part by their own choices, and in part because of the narrowly defined duties of those who held up the safety net.

In his richly descriptive study of what he terms the "legal consciousness of the welfare poor," Professor Austin Sarat casts light on the relationships between poor Americans and government institutions. His study documents the complex dance that takes place between state agencies designed to serve the poor and their clients. Using interviews with legal assistance clients (to whom he refers as "the welfare poor"), he demonstrates the manner in which Americans receiving public assistance manifest a dual sense of being both bound by the legal system and engaged in resistance against it: "[T]he legal consciousness of the welfare poor is a consciousness of power and domination, in which the keynote is enclosure and dependency, and a consciousness of resistance, in which welfare recipients assert themselves and demand recognition of their personal identities and their human needs."[1]

The women we interviewed manifested similarly complicated relationships with the government institutions that bounded their lives. The women worked in a deliberate manner to navigate through or around their encounters with various public agencies, attempting to avoid those that they perceived as threatening, while accepting the involvement of others as inevitable, or even as desirable.

Childhood Encounters with the State

The earliest awareness of the state, for most of the women with whom we spoke, involved the power of the government to take away the people they loved, or, worse, to take them away from their loved ones. Although almost none of the women had criminal records outside of their difficulties, as mothers, with Child Protective Services, many knew of people, in some cases family members, who were incarcerated. Others knew children who had been in the foster care system or they had been in it themselves.

These women were not unusual in developing an early awareness that the state serves a custodial function; children commonly are curious about jail; being locked up for punishment is a central feature in many childhood games. What was particularly interesting in these women's stories is the way in which they viewed the state as menacing, rather than protective.

The Foster Care System

Most of the women with whom we spoke were physically and emotionally abused and/or neglected as children.[2] Had the state been notified of their victimization, it would have investigated, and at least in some cases, it would have taken temporary or even permanent custody of these women and their siblings. For instance, in Vanessa's case, there is little doubt that the state would have taken her from her parents had it discovered that she was, at age ten, largely responsible for running her household and caring for her four younger half siblings. Similarly, the physical and emotional abuse in Nancy's mother's home, and in Nadine's father's home, would have been cause to remove them from their respective households.

In some cases, the state did intervene to assume custody of these women when they were children. These women typically did not recall the intervention as having been helpful. One of the women we interviewed told the following story about her experience with Child Protective Services:

> When I was eighteen months old my mother left me with a babysitter and moved to another state with her boyfriend. After three days the babysitter called child welfare and me and my brother were placed in foster care. When they eventually found my mother, she served six months for child endangerment. When my mother was released, we went to live with my stepfather, a recovering alcoholic, and my mother, an alcoholic. As a child, I witnessed violence between them. . . . I was also physically abused. When I was nine years old, my mother accused me of having sex and beat me with a belt and buckle. My father would point guns at my head when I did not eat meals. I was burnt with an iron twice and had tried suicide three times by the time I was eighteen years old. My family appeared "normal" in public. My mother told me all families were abusive even if they did not seem like it. She said that the abuse occurs "behind closed doors."

In spite of the history of abuse, Child Protective Services never again intervened to protect this woman. Indeed, she did not know that she had ever been in state custody until years later, when she was detained for neglecting her own child and a social worker recognized her name.

The best, or perhaps merely the least worst story of the state as a guardian of child welfare was told by Julie. Julie, three of whose children perished in a fire in her home, while she watched from outside, was taken from her parents' home at age two, along with her one-year-old sister. The girls remained together in foster care until Julie was five, when they were adopted as a sibling set. Julie has little positive to say about her adoptive parents:

> The only time my childhood was happy was when I was with my grandmother. I would call her and ask if I could spend weekends with

her. She knew something wasn't right because that child wants to get out of the house. I was the one who did all the work. I cooked and cleaned and had to do my homework. All my [sister] had to do was feed the dog.

It should not surprise us that the women did not tend to view Child Protective Services as a safe haven. Anyone familiar with state child welfare agencies knows that their capacity for protecting children is limited as a result of perennial budgetary constraints, which in turn result in excessively high case loads for undertrained case workers.[3] Beginning in the 1980s, numerous lawsuits have resulted in judgments against state child welfare agencies.[4] Children in foster care have been abused and neglected. Most children in the system, particularly those who are not placed with family members, do not find permanent placements, but instead are moved through a variety of placements, sometimes with, but more often without their siblings.[5] Indeed, the foster care system in some states is so overwhelmed that it has lost track of its wards completely.[6] From a savvy child's perspective, it is evident that being placed in foster care is far from a guarantee that one will be safe.

The fact that these women knew, as children, that Child Protective Services would not necessarily protect them, helps us to understand the emotional landscape of their daily lives. They were not safe at home, and yet, they had little hope that they would find safety anywhere else. The luckiest among them had perhaps one trusted adult to whom they could turn, on occasion, for reprieve. Vanessa, for instance, had a grandmother whom she could call: "Being young like that, [I had] some questions; [I'd] ask Grannie. Parties and holidays, she would ask if I wanted to participate. Took us places. She was wonderful." But her grandmother could not, or would not, make a permanent home for Vanessa and her four younger siblings. Ultimately, Vanessa was left with the task of running her family's home, and trying make things "seem normal."

Likewise, Nadine was able to rely, at least occasionally, on her grandfather, who permitted her to stay with him when her father abused or abandoned her. But he tired of caring for her and her brother and wanted to place the children in foster care:

My grandfather had had enough and called Children's Service Bureau. Mom was too far away. My brother was a handful and a half, especially after the car accident. I decided not to live in foster care. The reason a foster parent has forty-five kids in one house is money. I went to a friend's house from school. Her mom said "What do you need?" [I told her and she] said OK, and I moved in. . . . I lived with my friend but they went to Indiana and moved to a weird town. [There were] eleven churches and eleven bars. [The] chief of police looked at me real funny and he scared me. The way he looked at me was not the right way to look at a child.

Nadine left Indiana and returned to her grandfather's home. He agreed, once again, to take her in.

Several things are worth noting in Nadine's response to the prospect of foster care. First, she believed that foster care was more of a money-making racket for adults than a system for protecting vulnerable children. She had heard rumors about households filled with forty-five wards and concluded that adults running such homes would not necessarily be motivated by a desire to protect. Of course, Nadine's basic information is incorrect: State laws regulate the number of wards that any one family can accept, and although there is some variation amongst the states in terms of the maximum number of wards that a foster parent can house, no state would permit a family to accept forty-five wards at one time.[7]

The manner in which Nadine conceptualizes the ambitions of those involved in child protection reveals much about her sense of the purpose and promise of public institutions. Nadine does not imagine that foster families might be motivated by altruism, rather than by greed. A private arrangement with her friend's family therefore seems more promising to her than does the idea of state-based care.

The end of her story, in which she moves with the family to a different state, and then decides that she is unsafe because the chief of police "looked at her real funny," seems, at first, to be unrelated to the rest of her story. From Nadine's perspective, though, it is relevant because it tells us even more about how she experienced state agents. Not only can they not be trusted to protect you, but worse, those empowered by the state may use their power to do you harm.

Regardless of their personal experiences with state child welfare agencies, these women concluded, long before they became parents themselves, that the state was not there to help mothers and children, but rather to serve a more punitive role. As Nancy remarked, "If women are scared to come to you, then you're not really there to help. Child neglect can't be helped by the threat of taking kids. Authority figures can't be trusted.

[There's] no actual help out there. Just [the] threat of child neglect."[8] This theme reemerged with a vengeance once the women became mothers themselves. But first, it is important to consider their interactions with several other public institutions.

Public Schools

The public school system represents a second realm of government authority to which all these women were exposed as children. Most of the women had little to say about school, other than noting that they went, and then they stopped going. Indeed, what was interesting about these women's encounters with the school system is the fact that many of them dropped out before finishing secondary school.[9] The majority never went back to complete their degrees.

Their departure from school did not reflect their dislike for education. Several of those who spoke about dropping out of school noted that they did so with regret. They left because the forces shaping their lives — such as their living situations and their family situations — interfered with their ability to attend. Nancy, for instance, was enrolled in an alternative "technical" high school prior to dropping out:

> I had a teacher but she cried when I dropped out. She said you have a writer's voice, you have potential. I gave it up because my mom and dad said. All the way to thirteen, [I was] in learning disabled classes with straight As. [I was] too smart so they put me in regular classes. When I was fifteen and a half, [my parents pulled me out, and said that I was] wasting taxpayer money and our time. [They were] hoping I would try to prove them different — reverse psychology.

The more common reason for leaving school was that the women (actually, girls) became mothers. Some struggled to complete school, even after having children. Vanessa, for instance, describes her determination to stay in school after the birth of her first child, when she was fourteen:

> I left [school for good] when I was seventeen. Didn't want to be one of those girls. [I had m]oved into my own two bedroom, living room place. I was struggling but I was trying. I had quit school but I had gotten back in school. I would keep up. There were only a few months I had a tutor. Got back in school on my own. I had goals: hair — I loved doing hair. [I wanted to get my] license and to become a manager.

Shortly thereafter, Vanessa had a second, and then a third child. With three children under the age of five, her dreams of becoming a licensed cosmetologist were placed on hold.

Once they had their first babies, most of the women with whom we spoke seemed to accept leaving school as inevitable. They gave in to the necessity of caring for their child and did not look back. Many were preoccupied with very immediate, pressing issues, such as finding housing for themselves and their children. For most of these women, dropping out was not really an interruption; they never had developed a long-term plan that included finishing high school.

This is not to say that the women we interviewed never regretted leaving school. Several, such as Nancy, reported being shamed by their partners, who bragged about having finished high school. From the perspective of women like Nadine, Patty, or Nancy, however, thinking about school in the immediate aftermath of having their first children would have been a luxury. Along with caring for their newborns, they had to worry about how to manage life with their violent partners. They did not have a safe place to live, and they did not have enough money to live on their own. Perhaps it was their lack of faith in public institutions, or maybe it was simply their lack of mentoring, that stopped them from finding a high school that would have permitted them to attend along with their babies. Such programs were common by the time these women had their babies. For these women, though, school was part of a long-term plan, at best. Typically, they were occupied with immediate problems, to which motherhood both contributed and also provided short-term solutions, such as a place to live, or at a more abstract level, a sense of love and connection.

The Health Care System

Of all the institutions with which the women we interviewed interacted, it was the health care system that generated the most ambivalent and even negative feelings. Throughout their lives, these women had limited access to health care. They typically visited doctors only when either they or a loved one was in crisis. As many lacked private insurance, their health care, when they obtained it, was provided at public hospitals or clinics, by doctors who did not know them. Even in times of true medical crisis, these women and their families often tended to avoid the health care system.

Childhood Visits with Doctors

In spite of the fact that many of them reported suffering childhood traumas that ordinarily would have triggered medical interventions, the women we interviewed seldom saw doctors. Several described experiencing suicidal tendencies as children, and yet, none of them received mental health treatment for depression or anxiety. These tendencies often went beyond mere fantasies and included taking knives into bed, drinking noxious fluids, and even attempting to use a gun. Nancy describes several violent encounters with her mother, including the one in which her mother called 911 in order to get emergency medical technicians to help stop Nancy from killing herself. According to her account, the emergency medical technicians treated the event as a household dispute and left the house when the fight stopped. No attempt was made to secure follow-up care for Nancy.

The relative infrequency of their encounters with doctors and nurses as children may be a reflection of the fact that their families lacked comprehensive access to health care. Indeed, until recent legislation mandated increased access to health care for children whose families could not afford insurance, poor children were among the most likely segments of the U.S. population to be uninsured.[10] Numerous studies reveal that the uninsured simply do not access the health care system as often, or as effectively, as those who have insurance.[11]

Pregnancy and Health Care Treatment

For women with comprehensive health insurance, pregnancy typically ushers in an extended set of encounters with health care professionals. Prenatal care, vital to enhancing the likelihood of healthy outcomes for mothers and babies, requires monthly checkups in the early months of pregnancy and then more frequent checkups as birth draws nearer. In the vast majority of cases, the women we interviewed described very limited, erratic encounters with health care providers during their pregnancies, even when they faced medical emergencies.

Several women reported suffering miscarriages — two after being beaten. In spite of descriptions that included pain and considerable blood loss, apparently none of these women sought medical care. Recall that Nadine described hemorrhaging from a miscarriage when she was fourteen years old. Neither her boyfriend, nor his family, nor even her own family, thought to take her to a doctor.

The stories told by these women about their pregnancy-related encounters with the health care system reveal a sense of powerlessness at the hands of others. Many failed to acknowledge their pregnancies, waiting for others to notice and take them to get care. This pattern is not uncommon among young women, who tend to delay prenatal care.[12]

The avoidance of health care also might reflect a broader strategy on the part of these pregnant young women. Although they experienced relatively little control over circumstances in their lives, they had surmised that a visit to the doctor might further destabilize things. In essence, an encounter with a doctor triggers the involvement of outsiders in one's life. Visiting the doctor risks making evident the reality of impending change and thus may set in motion events that move one's life completely out of one's control.

For instance, recall Nadine's account of her father and his girlfriend's attempt to resolve the problem of her pregnancy with her oldest child, when she was fifteen. After learning that her pregnancy was too advanced for her to obtain an abortion, they arranged for her to relinquish the child to adoptive parents. A health care provider should have worked carefully with Nadine, alone and apart from her father (who plainly wanted her to abort or place the baby for adoption), to determine whether Nadine was comfortable with these choices. According to her story, though, Nadine was not consulted by the health care providers involved in her care. It is not clear whether this conversation did not happen because Nadine did not trust her health care providers, and therefore said nothing to them, or rather because they did not honor their legal and ethical obligations to Nadine, as their patient, by insuring that she was making a confidential, autonomous choice. Instead, Nadine defied her parents and her health care providers by leaving the hospital after her baby's premature delivery, prior to signing the adoption papers. Several days later, with her grandfather's help, she returned to the hospital and brought her baby home. Nadine did not report feeling empowered by this set of encounters with the health care system. From her perspective, things had been stable for the first twenty-five weeks of her pregnancy, when no one knew about it except for her. The involvement of others did not bring her comfort, but rather stress and grief.

Another set of pregnancy-related stories speaks to the women's perceptions that the health care system cannot be trusted and that it offers only limited assistance. Concealed or denied pregnancies involve women who, for a variety of reasons, fear acknowledging their pregnancies to

anyone. Typically, they carry their pregnancies without obtaining any prenatal care, and they deliver their babies alone, often in a bathroom. Laurie's story was in some ways quite typical of neonaticide, although unlike
most women who commit this crime, she already was a mother and had
experienced several pregnancies before the one that ended in homicide.

Recall that Laurie became pregnant when a friend of the family raped
her. She did not seek medical treatment, nor did she notify the police
about the rape. She was terrified of the consequences that might follow
from disclosing the rape and her rapist's identity. "I was scared," she said:

> [t]o see what my step dad would have done. When he's angry. He
> would have confronted the guy—beat the crap out of him. Could
> have killed him. Called the sheriff. Denied it for so long. I should have
> done something. I was scared he'd deny it. People would look down on
> me. [My] son [is] in school. I cared about what would be said about
> me or my family. They would think less of me, kick me out of house.

Her fear of disclosure led her to avoid the health care system, as she was
convinced that they would have revealed her secret. Laurie had little confidence that she could find assistance in the health care system. Perhaps she
was not aware of her rights to confidentiality, which would have obligated
her health care providers to protect her secrets. Or perhaps she avoided
the health care system because getting prenatal care would have made
both the rape and her ensuing pregnancy seem more real, and she would
have been forced to take action.

Mothering and Interactions with the Health Care System

As they moved into motherhood, the tendency to avoid and distrust
the health care system seemed to intensify for the women we interviewed.
They, along with their children, spent little time interacting with doctors.
The absence of routine postpartum and pediatric health care visits may
seem strange from the perspective of those who enjoy health insurance
and view the health care system as a partner in their family's health. Mothers often worry, and the role of pediatricians typically is to assess those
worries, assuring that one's child is developing normally.

From the perspective of the women with whom we spoke, a visit
to the health care system was fraught with risk. The health care system
represents, in many ways, the front line in terms of prevention of child
abuse and neglect. Health care providers have an opportunity to identify

children at risk of harm, to observe parents in order to determine the extent to which they are coping with the tasks of child rearing, to make referrals for assistance, and to be a resource for parents who are struggling. There is the promise of help in this mission, and yet, because the law mandates that health care providers report suspected child abuse, these women correctly understood that they could not count on their children's doctors to be their loyal allies. They feared losing their children and ultimately, all control over their lives, by being judged harshly by their health care providers.

Their fears were not irrational. For a variety of reasons, the health care providers who treated these women defined their jobs narrowly. Take Nancy's case as an example. Two weeks after her daughter's birth, Nancy brought her baby to a local public hospital for a routine checkup. She talked to the nurse about the fact that she was crying every day, at times inconsolably. The nurse talked to her about postpartum depression, but there was no follow-up to this conversation. According to Nancy, the nurse did not ask about her living situation, and so she never learned that Nancy had no place to live with her two small children — a fact that surely was exacerbating Nancy's depression. The nurse completed her primary task by giving the baby a two-week checkup, in which she determined that the baby was thriving, although she was a half pound underweight. Nancy was not given a referral for mental health services.

Nancy might have been comforted to know that her sadness had a diagnosis, but given the more pressing difficulties in her life, it was highly unrealistic to imagine that she would have taken the initiative to obtain treatment for her problem. It was only after she was incarcerated that Nancy was diagnosed with bipolar disorder and began to receive medication to help stabilize her moods.

It is neither unusual, nor irrational, for health care providers to define narrowly the scope of their duties. To the extent that a health care provider construes her obligations to her patient very broadly — to encompass, say, the patient's mental health, or the stability and safety of her living situation — the complexity of the task of treating a patient multiplies. Moreover, health care providers are not necessarily trained, or paid, to spot, treat, and make referrals to other providers for health problems stemming from broad social problems such as domestic violence or even mental health issues.[13]

The U.S. health care system is diagnosis and treatment driven, and for reasons ranging from reimbursement mechanisms to fear of medical malpractice, doctors tend to limit the scope of their duties. Under the current system, it is unrealistic to look to health care providers as resources for linking vulnerable individuals and families to local agencies. If they lack an ongoing relationship with a seemingly vulnerable patient or her family, there is a much stronger incentive for them to file a report with Child Protective Services than there is to try to encourage the woman to seek help. It is a crime for a health care provider to fail to report suspected child abuse or neglect; it is merely a shame to fail to make appropriate referrals to agencies such as day care providers, mental health care providers, or battered women's shelters.

Nancy's description of taking her newborn for a checkup is unusual not because the nurse failed to make mental health referrals, but rather because she visited the nurse in the first place. Most of the women with whom we spoke did not recount obtaining such routine care for their babies. Instead, the only routine encounters their babies had with health care providers tended to happen at home, after the women had been reported for suspected child abuse or neglect and been assigned case workers. Their stories tended to reveal a vicious cycle, in which their fear of the health care system led them to avoid obtaining medically necessary care for their children, which in turn led to their being reported for child abuse or neglect. This pattern played out multiple times in these women's lives.

Two stories are particularly illustrative of the avoidance of the health care system and the crises that may be precipitated by such avoidance. First, recall Vanessa's story. Angered by her child's threat to "tell Daddy" that Vanessa's boyfriend was hitting her and the other children, Vanessa hit her child and broke her arm. Instead of bringing her to the hospital, she did her best to set the arm on her own, because "children's services was just going to take your kid." Ultimately, she was reported to Child Protective Services for failing to obtain medical care for her daughter, and her child was temporarily taken from her. No more than two years later, reunited with her children, Vanessa again faced a situation in which a child needed medical care, and again she refused to take her daughter to the hospital. This time, her daughter had been scalded. Vanessa maintains that she simply did not think her daughter was severely injured. Vanessa's decision was influenced by her perception that a hospital visit was fraught with the risk of losing custody of her children.

Nadine's story also helps to illustrate the manner in which these women perceived the health care system. After she returned home from work to find her seven-year-old son lying unconscious, having been beaten by her husband, Mack, Nadine did not call 911. Her husband prevented her from calling anyone by tearing the phone from the wall. The terror of this story obscures the puzzling nature of the plan of action that Nadine later described as having devised for herself and her children while sitting beside her dying child:

> He ripped the phone out of my hand and whupped my ass. Told me to dry him off and get dry clothes on him. I planned when he woke up and [Mack]'s gone we're leaving. I was waiting on a paycheck. Told God to please wake him up. Told God it was bad enough he beats on me. . . . [I was] trying to decide how to get away. Other kids come in and Mack tells them Josh is sick. I hold his hand praying [Mack] will go to sleep. I fell asleep before [Mack] did.

Even in the throes of this medical emergency, Nadine's plan did not include taking her child to a hospital. She planned on leaving and was trying to decide how, and where to go, but she was not working on figuring out how to get her son to a doctor. It simply did not occur to her that a hospital was likely to provide her with the help that she and her children needed. Their needs were too big, and, like many battered women, she did not trust the health care providers to keep her best interests in mind.

Nadine's and Vanessa's stories about avoiding the health case system were not unusual. The children of two of the women we interviewed died from fevers. Neither sought medical help; both admitted that they avoided getting emergency care for their ill child because they feared that this intervention would lead to their losing custody of all their children.

Public Assistance

Over the course of their lives, the majority of the women we interviewed were, at least on occasion, welfare recipients. Until the "welfare reform" of the mid-1990s, relatively long-term public aid was available to unmarried women who needed help supporting their children.[14] This assistance came in the form of grants, and also via access to subsidized low-income housing.

Public assistance came with a number of price tags, though. Among these was a sense of stigma associated with being on welfare. The political rhetoric of the late twentieth century shamed women who relied on public assistance to support themselves and their children.[15] In a well-known epithet, President Ronald Reagan referred to such mothers as "welfare queens."[16]

Resentment of lazy, manipulative Americans who are perceived as living "on the dole" has given rise to what essentially is a two-tier social welfare system.[17] The "deserving poor" are disproportionately men, who rely on relatively generous, long-term, and secure benefits, such as social security, disability payments, or unemployment compensation. In contrast, the "undeserving poor" receive welfare, in the form of short-term, conditional benefits — like Temporary Assistance for Needy Families (TANF). The latter tend overwhelmingly to be women and children, and rather than qualifying as a matter of course, as one does for social security or unemployment compensation, their benefits are administered by local officials who exercise a great deal of discretion.[18]

On occasion, the women we interviewed echoed these popular perceptions of welfare recipients, making it plain that they had heard, and to some extent adopted this perspective on public assistance. For example, Marlene commented that her conviction and relatively long prison sentence resulted, in part, from the negative public response to her living situation: "[I was] nineteen when [my] first was born; twenty when I had [my] second. Living on my own, on welfare, no 'skills.' Had I been normal, married . . . [it] might have helped." Similarly, Vanessa echoed some of the conventional understanding of welfare when she noted that "I know girls that use kids to have welfare."

When they referred to their personal experiences with welfare, as opposed to the general perception of welfare recipients, these women described themselves in a manner that was almost completely at odds with the popular imagery. Rather than internalizing a sense of shame about receiving public aid, these women viewed welfare as one of the systems that enabled them to contend with their most pressing needs — food and shelter. Welfare was not part of a long-term plan; rather, it was something they relied on in a crisis, to help them to escape intolerable relationships, and to achieve some stability for themselves and their children.

Contrary to the popular image of the lifelong welfare-dependent mother, these women tended to move onto and off of the welfare rolls with some frequency, typically as a result of their fluctuating living relationships with their partners. (In order to qualify for Aid to Families with Dependent Children, one needed to demonstrate that there was no other source of financial support in the household. Thus, the presence of a second breadwinner in the house was grounds for terminating aid.[19])

In his ethnographic study of women on welfare, *American Dream: Three Women, Ten Kids, and a Nation's Drive to End Welfare,* Jason De Parle documents this on-and-off pattern. He finds that, although some women are quite strategic in their attempts to manipulate the system (for instance, one was unabashed about her motivations for moving to Milwaukee because welfare there "pays the most"), most are fighting to get out of poverty and to maintain a sense of dignity at the same time.[20]

The struggle to maintain one's dignity was not inconsistent with receiving public assistance. Indeed, the stories told by the women we interviewed revealed that there was more pride than shame associated with obtaining welfare. For instance, Vanessa noted that, prior to obtaining welfare, "I felt like I was in an 'I can't win for losing' situation." She and her baby were moving back and forth between her grandmother's home and her parents' home, she was attempting to stay in high school, working a job after school, caring for her younger siblings, and trying to conceal her parents' substance abuse from others. When her second and third children were born, her fear of being found unfit as a parent, and thereby losing custody of her children, led her to seek public assistance so that she could move into her own apartment: "My biggest thing was not getting them taken away. I left [home] when I was seventeen. . . . Moved into my own two-bedroom, living room place. I was struggling but I was trying. . . . I felt like I was independent."

From the perspective of one who has never been on public assistance, Vanessa's sense of independence while on welfare may seem ironic. One might reason that among the highest price tags associated with receiving public assistance is the dependence it implies and the loss of autonomy and privacy it entails. In his study of the "welfare poor," Professor Sarat suggests that, when compared to more privileged members of society, those who receive public assistance tend to have different sensibilities and expectations regarding privacy, particularly when it comes to the role of government in their lives. He describes the ubiquitous presence of the law in the lives of those who receive public assistance:

> Law is, for people on welfare, repeatedly encountered in the most ordinary transactions and events of their lives. Legal rules and practices are implicated in determining whether and how welfare recipients will

be able to meet some of their most pressing needs. . . . [B]eing on welfare means having a significant part of one's life organized by a regime
of legal rules invoked by officials to claim jurisdiction over choices
and decisions which those not on welfare would regard as personal
and private.[21]

Sarat argues that recipients of public aid tolerate the law's intrusive-
ness; indeed, they have an entirely different view of the role of law in their
lives than do non-recipients because they are engaged in a simultaneous
process of reliance on and resistance to the bureaucracy. He describes the
manner in which the "ongoing series of transactions with officials visibly
engaged in the interpretation and use of rules" primes public aid recipients with knowledge and skills that enable them to "respond strategically,
to maneuver and to resist" the bureaucrats, so that the system better meets
their needs.[22]

The women with whom we spoke seemed to exemplify Sarat's description of resistance. Welfare did not define them; it was there for them
as an occasional foothold in an unstable world.

Child Protection Agencies

A disturbing number of the women incarcerated for having killed their
children had been investigated and even sanctioned, prior to the events
that led to their children's deaths, by state Child Protective Services agencies. Over one-third of the women with whom we spoke acknowledged
that the state had investigated them at some point for allegations of child
abuse or neglect; more than a few had temporarily lost custody of their
children. One might therefore read these stories as indictments of state
child protection agencies, using these cases to substantiate the claim that
these agencies routinely fail to identify children who are truly at risk of
harm, and that they are too hesitant when it comes to permanently re-
moving children from the custody of incompetent parents and dangerous
households.

Although there is a plausible critique that may be brought against child
protection agencies for their failure to adequately differentiate households
that might be rehabilitated and rendered safe for children from those that
are unlikely to be rendered safe, even after receiving support services, our
interviews should not be read as supporting that critique. Such a claim

would require a larger sample of cases than we provide here — a sample in which one might consider these cases of fatal abuse following reunification in the context of all cases of reunification. In short, what we have here is a numerator — cases in which there were fatalities, in spite of prior state agency involvement — but no denominator.

Instead, we learn a different lesson from these cases. As we have seen, perhaps the greatest fear in the lives of these women was the threat of losing custody of their children. Interestingly, those women who actually experienced this threat, and who were subjected to official investigation and in some cases to temporary loss of custody, often experienced the state's intervention into their lives as a positive, rather than negative occurrence.

There are at least two ways in which the encounters between these women and child protection workers emerged as positive. The first is that a caseworker occasionally provided a mother with positive feedback or a sense of validation. This was the case with Nancy, whose stepcousins reported her to the Department of Social Services, she believes, because "they were trying to adopt [her] baby." As a result of the report, the state opened an investigation into Nancy's parenting skills. The only thing they ever found wrong with her baby, according to Nancy, was that her daughter was slightly underweight. Nancy regrets that the nurse, the pediatrician, and the head Department of Social Services case supervisor were not called to testify at her trial. "All of them could've told how she checked out and was found to be fine," she said.

Nancy's interactions with the state case worker presented her with a rare opportunity for praise. Not only did she express a sense of relief that she was not ruled unfit as a mother, Nancy felt proud when the caseworker found that her baby was safe and healthy. The nurse may well have been the only adult to offer her any validation of her work as a mother. And her work as a mother was considerable: Nancy spent long hours, without the support of other adults, attending to all of the basic needs of both of her children. She was lonely, exhausted, and hungry for the praise of someone whom she respected.

Vanessa's story also illustrates the extent to which the relationships between the women and their state child protection caseworkers might be positive, rather than negative. From the time she had her first child, Vanessa was deeply worried about the risk of losing custody. "[I] knew a lot who, after child services called, they'd nine times out of ten take your kids," she said. Ironically, when she was convicted of criminal neglect for having failed to obtain necessary medical treatment for her four-year-old daughter, she developed a meaningful relationship with her caseworker, whom she recalled warmly.

As punishment for child neglect, Vanessa served thirty days in jail and had to take a parenting class and have supervised visits with her children. With the help of her caseworker, Vanessa regained custody: "[My] caseworker warned me that I was 'under a microscope' and that any little thing that I'd do wrong, they'd take the baby. [The caseworker] would come, check that things were fine. [She] checked at school, with and without notice. [She] gave lots of feedback, and let me know when I was doing things right or wrong."

Recall that Vanessa was the oldest of five children of drug-addicted parents. As such, these routine meetings with her caseworker may have been the first positive mentoring she received in terms of parenting techniques. She learned to try time-outs and taking away television and toy privileges, rather than whippings, when disciplining her children. She received praise, as well as criticism. And she seemed to enjoy the feeling that somebody was watching out for her, even though that feeling was accompanied by a warning.

The child protection officers also helped the women to gain some stability. The women who temporarily lost custody of their children were given very specific, concrete tasks that they needed to complete in order to be reunited with their children. The women were, understandably, highly motivated in undertaking these tasks. And from their descriptions, they did not see the tasks as meaningless. Whether they were discussing parenting classes or the search for stable employment and housing, the fact that they had a case worker and a set goal seemed to anchor them, providing them with an exit from their violent relationships and guiding them toward a more stable future. For example, after the Children's Services Bureau took custody of the children, Nadine lost her government-funded housing and her welfare. This led her to leave her husband, move in with a friend, and find a job. Working with her caseworker, she made a plan for reunification: "find a home, stop using [drugs.] . . . I was trying to get stable. I was taking parenting classes, [I] had a caseworker."

At one level, it is ridiculous to talk about the positive aspects of the relationship between child protection caseworkers and these mothers. Because these women were later implicated in their children's deaths, these relationships would seem, by definition, to have failed. It is important to examine the reasons why these relationships failed at their central task. At the same time, though, it is important to see the potential that these relationships had to transform the manner in which these women were raising their children.

Even more than in the case of their interactions with health care workers, there is a sense of missed opportunity when considering the relationships between these women and their caseworkers. Because these women tended to trust and respect their caseworkers, their connections represented the best opportunity for preventing the tragedies that ultimately took their children's lives. For example, consider the impact that Nancy's nurse caseworker might have had, if only she had construed her obligations a bit more broadly. Her caseworker seems to have undertaken a narrow investigation, checking only to see that the baby was healthy, rather than noticing that Nancy and her children did not have a stable home, that she was depressed, and that she was subjected to emotional and physical abuse at the hands of her mother. Had she undertaken even a slightly broader inquiry into Nancy's well-being, Nancy's distress would have been evident. The caseworker could have helped Nancy to access local resources such as mental health services, welfare, and housing support. Such services likely would have helped to stabilize Nancy's family's life, which could have been instrumental in preventing harm to her children.

In the other cases, though, it is harder to blame the children's deaths on the caseworkers' errors. Nadine's caseworker began working with her only after Nadine was separated from her first partner. Their time together was devoted to developing and carrying out a reunification plan. Nadine was single during this time, so her caseworker likely did not recognize the extent to which she was drawn to abusive relationships, which put her and her children at risk. Nadine regained custody shortly after she met and moved in with her the violent man who ultimately killed her child.

Perhaps the caseworker might be faulted for failing to investigate the reality that underlay Nadine's comfort in her relationship with her new partner, who promised to support her basic needs. To one with some familiarity with the patterns surrounding domestic violence, Nadine's descriptions of her new partner would have raised concerns. He was an unemployed "regular" at the bar where she worked, who had been married four times before, and who was on probation due to a conviction for battering his ex-wife. These factors might have suggested that he posed considerable risk to Nadine and her children. Nonetheless, until there was evidence that he was actually harming Nadine or the children, it would have been unduly harsh to preclude reunification on the basis that he seemed likely to become abusive in the future.[23]

Unfortunately, by the time that Nadine recognized the vulnerability in her new relationship, her case had been closed, and she no longer had a relationship with her caseworker. She lacked a trusted mentor or confidante. Because the foundation that underlies the relationship between a caseworker and a parent is punitive in nature, it is readily terminated once the parent completes the agreed-upon course of action. As such, Nadine's successful completion of her parenting and reunification program left her as isolated and bereft of confidantes and allies as she had been in her first relationship.

The death of Vanessa's child from medical neglect is even more difficult to link to the negligence of the child protection caseworker. At first blush, it seems easy to fault the caseworker, as Vanessa's distrust of the health care system was to blame both for her original child abuse conviction and also for the later death of her child. One might think that the caseworker should have anticipated that Vanessa would once again put her children at risk by her inclination to avoid health care providers. Such reasoning merely restates the ironic tautology that dominated Vanessa's life: her top priority was keeping custody of her children, which led her to avoid any entity that she perceived as a threat to that priority, even if it might have helped her children. In light of this priority, one can understand how Vanessa came to view the relationship with her caseworker as a positive one; her caseworker had the power to help Vanessa get her children back and keep them in her life. Vanessa came to see her caseworker as her advocate, one who could see how much she loved her daughters and how hard she was willing to work to have them with her. Because the relationship between Vanessa and her caseworker was bounded by the punitive nature of the child welfare system, however, once Vanessa completed her reunification tasks, their connection was severed. Once again, she came to view all her interactions with public officials as hazardous.

The positive relationships that these women reported with their caseworkers may be simply an artifact of the power structure that underlay these relationships. Their caseworkers had the capacity to ratify their abilities as mothers and to reunify them with their children. From the perspective of an individual who has never been the subject of a child protection investigation, it might seem preposterous to suggest that these interactions might be genuinely positive. But given these women's life experiences, this conclusion is not necessarily warranted. Institutions that typically seem like resources to those with more privilege in their lives (e.g., hospitals) seemed threatening to these women. So too institutions predicated on punishment (e.g., child welfare agencies) nonetheless often proved to be a source of support.

Several lines of research support the positive sense of these interactions that was conveyed by the women with whom we spoke.[24] Professor Laurie MacKinnon, the author of *Trust and Betrayal in the Treatment of Child Abuse*, and an expert on parenting and child abuse, observed the potential for meaningful relationships to develop between mothers and caseworkers: "In situations where parents initiate contact with the Department or consent to the referral, the relationship that develops with the child protection authorities is less adversarial. These parents are much more likely than involuntary clients to perceive their child protection workers as 'friends.'"[25] MacKinnon notes that even among those who are identified by the state, rather than initiating contact on their own, to the extent that the state can provide tangible solutions to specific problems in their lives, there is a great potential for collaboration.[26] Advocates for child protection reform stress the extent to which a punitive model alienates the very clients one hopes to reach. Thus, they argue in favor of "providing services to marginally dysfunctional families, and doing so by truly offering families help — not ultimatums or demands to admit to something they did not do."[27]

The stories told by the women we interviewed demonstrate a hopeful potential for collaboration between agents of the child welfare system and vulnerable families. For those who are as marginalized and isolated as were the women with whom we spoke, caseworkers can fill a significant void. With adequate training and resources, these state agents might prove to be trusted mentors who can work with these mothers toward the goal of long-term stability.

Interactions with the Criminal Justice System

The final public institution with which the women whom we interviewed came into contact was the criminal justice system. The women encountered officials and agents of the criminal justice system throughout their lives, whether in the form of police, probation officers, lawyers, or judges. Legally speaking, there are such significant distinctions between the various actors who compose the criminal justice system — for instance, between defense lawyers and prosecutors — that generic terms such as "the law" are almost meaningless. For the women with whom we spoke,

however, "the law" was not merely ubiquitous; it also was viewed as a sin-
gular, uniform, and typically corrupt entity. This emerges most clearly in
their descriptions of the lawyers involved in their homicide cases.

Many of the women we interviewed felt distrustful of their lawyers.
This was true whether they were served by public defenders, who were
employed by the state, or by private defense lawyers. Vanessa, for instance,
had deep scorn for her lawyers: "At the time I thought they were on my
side. [She was a] 'Public Pretender.'[28] She had never done a murder case.
Sided with [the prosecutor]." She also railed against her lawyers for failing to involve more of her family members in her defense at trial, as she
believed that their testimony might have mitigated the severity of her
sentence.

Nancy's mother paid $150 an hour, according to Nancy, so that she
could have private defense lawyers. She regards as a waste her mother's effort to secure higher-quality legal representation by paying for private lawyers. According to Nancy, the lawyers failed to subpoena witnesses who
might have testified to her devotion and ability as a mother. For instance,
she notes that her lawyers did not locate the officials who had investigated
and dismissed the allegations of child abuse against her. She felt insulted
by her lawyers' treatment of her, and she even seemed to conflate her defense lawyers' actions with those of the prosecution:

> They asked me questions and told me what was going on. Tried to file
> [a claim of] incompetence. Tried to say the baby was shaken. I never
> shook my child. I told them I had proof I never shook a child. I told
> her to subpoena [the baby's] birth records. It was a traumatized birth.
> [The] whites around the eyes were red. I don't know if that caused
> hairline fracture. Then people got on the stand on behalf of the state.
> . . . [They said] . . . I had no emotion . . . the pediatrician [could have]
> explained to them — urgent care — but they would not subpoena him.

Not only did Nancy feel that her lawyers had misjudged her, but more
generally, she did not view them as her advocates. Perhaps the most telling thing about Nancy's perception of her lawyers was the fact that she
did not feel that she could trust them with the information that she had
become pregnant while awaiting trial. She believed that her lawyers would
force her to abort the pregnancy: "It took ninety days to bring me into the
trial. [The] lawyers advised terminating pregnancy. 'Wouldn't look good

being pregnant.'" So Nancy avoided the lawyers until she was five months pregnant. "After five months," she said, "they couldn't touch me."

Many of the women with whom we spoke conveyed their sense that they could not trust their lawyers. As one woman related:

> During my discovery, I did tell my attorneys how I committed my crime but I did not go into anything about trying to kill myself or the sixteen-year-old raping me in front of my children and threatening them. I gave them the bare basics and much less than I have given you [referring to the interviewer]. . . . At first it was trust — they were court appointed — what were they fighting for anyway? I had two court-appointed attorneys from out of state — one had served time previously as a prosecutor.

A client's failure to be forthcoming with her defense lawyer, owing to her distrust of the lawyer or of the entire criminal justice system, often impedes the lawyer's ability to provide a thorough defense. In several of our cases, this distrust of the system, and the failure to tell the full story to their lawyers, lent an air of self-fulfilling prophesy to the ultimate judgment rendered against the women. For instance, because she was ashamed to disclose that she had been raped, Laurie's lawyers did not know that her impulse to hide her pregnancy likely was a symptom of rape trauma syndrome.[29] Moreover, the jury was not permitted to consider the extent to which the circumstances surrounding the pregnancy mitigated the severity of her crime.

Much of the conflict between defense lawyers and their clients stems from misperceptions and failures in communication. The following story, told by one of the women, demonstrates the distrust she experienced in her relationship with her lawyer, who she faulted for failing to call, ignoring her legal arguments, and being "friendly" with "the other side":

> Well, I only talked to my lawyer two times from March to December. He never returned my phone calls and he guaranteed me that I wouldn't get any time. . . . He asked me about what happened only one time. . . . When we went to court, the prosecutor was saying all these things about me and he didn't say anything on my behalf. He didn't even put in any of my legal work . . . he didn't defend me at all . . . he didn't say that my kids were taken care of. No one in the family

had been in trouble before. . . . My grandma kept paying him money
. . . basically, we just listened to him and I got all that time.

It is possible that the women we interviewed felt differently about
their lawyers prior to their convictions. Likewise, it may be that their sense
that "the law" is a single, monolithic institution is a product, in part, of
their disappointment with the outcome of their case. As is the case with
many prison inmates, the women we interviewed tended to believe that
their convictions reflected a miscarriage of justice. Many of the women
spoke in detail about their belief that the state had misconstrued the evidence against them. Some admitted to harming their babies by neglect,
but they were outraged by the allegations of child abuse. In at least a few
of the cases, their protestations of innocence seemed plausible to us.[30]

From the perspective of those we interviewed, as well as from our
own, one of the most powerful critiques of the legal system lay in the in-
consistency of outcomes in factually similar cases. Patty raised this argu-
ment when comparing her relatively long sentence to those received by
more affluent women: "The only thing [evidence] that they had against
me was my character. . . . If I'd known contacts, had parents with money, I
could've gotten out. . . . And [the] public wouldn't have looked down on
me as much."

Nadine questioned the fairness of the sentence she received — twenty-
five years — for failing to protect her son from her abusive husband.
Her husband, who killed her child and then threatened to harm Nadine
and her other children if they disclosed his death, received only a fifteen-
year-to-life sentence. Even if one agrees that the failure to intervene to
stop a killing should be treated the same as actually killing, it is difficult to
justify the fact that Nadine's husband, who beat and killed her child, received a sentence than is, at least potentially, ten years shorter than
Nadine's.

Some cases are particularly hard to compare to others, making it difficult to evaluate the women's allegations of injustice and corruption. Others
more readily lend themselves to comparison. One case stood out from the
others in this regard: Laurie's fifteen-year-to-life sentence in the neonaticide death of her newborn baby. Past research into the crime of neonaticide reveals that, in most cases, this crime is understood as being distinct
from other forms of maternal filicide.[31] There is some evidence suggesting
that those who commit neonaticide tend to receive shorter sentences than
do mothers who kill older children.[32] Indeed, several other Ohio women

were convicted of similar crimes, yet received far shorter sentences in the same prison during the years that Laurie has been imprisoned.[33]

In the end, what seemed to bother the women at least as much as their sense of being judged unfairly was the feeling that they had been objectified by the officials they encountered within the criminal justice system. Woman after woman expressed a sense of having been silenced. Their stories did not get told; no one seemed to care about their perspectives on their lives and on their children's deaths. As one woman from our first set of interviews said of her lawyer, "He did not listen to half of what I said. He didn't let me answer the questions."

Conclusion

The institutions discussed in this chapter typically are not viewed as part of a single entity. It may seem odd, at first, to think about the health care system or the public schools as part of the government's power structure, which, along with the criminal justice system or the welfare system, sits in judgment of those who would violate its norms. Those with more power and privilege are far more likely to view public agencies according to the benefits they afford, rather than the threats they pose.

From the perspective of these women, though, the state was a unified entity. It was ubiquitous and judgmental, untrustworthy and unsympathetic. Little good could come of an encounter with any public official; indeed, each encounter, whether with a police officer, a physician, a teacher, or a caseworker, carried with it the possibility of harm. The women tended to view those who worked in any capacity for the state as having power that might be exercised, arbitrarily or not, unwittingly or intentionally, in order to destabilize their fragile hold on their lives.

The stories told in this chapter offer a new perspective on state agencies and actors. In addition, they provide a wide-angled lens through which we might glimpse, anew, the profound isolation and hopelessness in these women's lives. The extent to which the government, in its various guises, failed to provide them with meaningful support merely compounded and reinforced the alienation that they already felt within their families and communities. Their isolation from others emerges in these stories as complete. They were alone with their children.

7

The End of the Story

WHEN WE EMBARKED upon this project, we consciously avoided asking the women to explain or defend their crimes. There was an optional question, in our first survey, that invited them to tell us, in their own words, what had happened. But we knew what they had done, or at least what the criminal justice system determined that they had done. We did not want to solicit their explanations; we anticipated that their stories about their children's deaths would be self-serving and not terribly helpful to us in our efforts to understand the circumstances that gave rise to their crimes. And, at some level, we simply did not want to hear this part of their stories because it was too terrible. But of course, their crimes were the focal points, the cores of their stories. The women carried them into the small room where we sat; they placed them before us with outstretched arms, avoiding our gaze, yet yearning for our empathy.

Their dead children seemed to hover up near the corners of the ceiling as we spoke. They followed us home, emerging at night, in our dreams, silent, eyes open, gazing at us. Were they asking us how we could have let this happen? Or were they simply watching us, waiting to see what we would to do with what we had learned?

We have endeavored here to honor the memory of these children, and the trust that their mothers placed in us, by serving as cautious witnesses. In this final chapter, we summarize what we have learned from the stories that these mothers shared with us, and we consider what the implications of these findings are for matters of justice and for reducing and preventing such crimes in the future.

Mothers Who Kill and Mothers Who Do Not: Lessons on Resilience

The stories that these women told us rippled with pain. Their childhoods were short; for the most part, the adults in their lives were inconstant and untrustworthy. Their choices, from an early age, reflected both a yearning for love and a need to control the emotional pain that came from its lack. Time and again, we were struck by the countless ways that their hearts had been broken.

When we had finished, and could hold the stories together, as if they were one entity, feeling their weight in our hands, holding them up to the light, we were struck as much by what we knew as by what we did not. There is no denominator, no frame of reference, for evaluating these women's experiences, because we have no information about mothers who also reached the brink of killing their children but somehow turned back. How far from the norm were these women's childhoods? Are others who survive such childhoods, and who attempt to parent in similar degrees of isolation, more resilient? And if so, what factors contribute to the others' resilience? Which of the many horrors these women shared with us is the critical one — the one that led inexorably to the deaths of their children?

It seems almost to go without saying that our effort to study women who kill their children is limited by the extent to which we have not, and cannot, truly study women who do not kill their children. Our years of gathering these stories, and of listening to mothers talk about their lives, have taught us that the line separating mothers who kill from those who do not is surprisingly blurry. Of course, the vast majority of mothers do not kill their children. Some never even consider it. But even a passing familiarity with these cases causes one to wonder about the way in which mothers who kill are like those who abuse or neglect their children, and about why it is that some mothers cope when others fail.

While we were researching our last book, and in the years since it was published, we have gathered more than a few "near miss" stories. Mothers have approached us, having learned of our project, and told us their stories. One Ohio woman, now in her sixties, told one of us the following story. She had worked while her husband attended medical school, and then, when he started his residency, they had a son. By mutual agreement, she quit her nursing career to stay home and parent. Soon they had two more boys. With the demands of his practice, her husband was rarely home, and she frequently acted as a single parent.

As time passed, they grew apart, and eventually, he told her that he had fallen in love with another woman and wanted a divorce. In addition, he informed her that he intended to petition for sole custody of the children. He had removed her name from joint checking accounts, so she had little access to money. Even if she could have found a job, two of the boys were still under five years old and would require daycare, which she could not afford. She had no relatives who lived near her who could provide her with respite care. Every time her husband picked up the children for visitation, she feared she would never see them again. After months of depression and anxiety, she figured out a solution: she would give the boys and herself an overdose of sleeping pills. She mixed the pills in with their ice cream one evening and was about to call them in for their snack when the phone rang. It was her pastor calling to see how she was coping. She threw the ice cream away. She was fortunate.

The women who recounted these "near miss" stories to us often identified one seemingly random event that saved them. Rather than sharing a concrete attribute or asset, such as an education, or access to health care, or even the absence of mental illness, the women pointed to serendipitous interventions: a phone call, a friend's visit, something that broke their solitude. From just a handful of anecdotes, it is impossible to make any sweeping generalizations. We did not, after all, set out to determine why mothers do not kill their children. Nor did we solicit these "near miss" stories. In fact, had we attempted to solicit them in a more formal research setting, we wonder how many of these women would have been forthcoming.

In an effort to understand why some mothers do not harm their children, in spite of the fact that their circumstances are similar to those described by the women we interviewed, one might look to the literature on resilience. The limited research that has been conducted on maternal resilience has focused on mothers of children with disabilities and mothers who live in risky environments. Mary Jane Weiss[1] found that hardiness and social support were predictive of successful adaptation in mothers of children with autism or mental retardation. Similarly, Trudy Horton[2] and Jan Wallander found that hope and social support decreased distress in mothers who were caring for children with chronic physical conditions. Finally, Cynthia Schellenbach and others[3] identified the need for a community based prevention partnership in order to build resilience among at-risk mothers.

Social support emerges as the key factor in increasing resilience. The absence of support is a constant factor underlying the various categories of mothers who kill their children, and connecting the stories we have gathered here. At their core, the stories of mothers who kill their children are stories about isolation, and the struggle to be a parent in the absence of a reliable community.

Responding to the Stories

In the end, then, we are left with the haunting question of how one might best respond to these stories. From the first, our response to them was fraught with ambivalence. The first and perhaps the most powerful impulse we felt was the need to distance ourselves from these women, denying even the possibility that we might be capable of such monstrous acts. There is a relative comfort in this position; one can listen to the stories as one might watch a horror film or a train wreck in slow motion. The sense of inevitable tragedy remains impersonal.

There is an undeniable psychic consolation to be found in simply exiling mothers who kill their children to the fringes of humanity. If they are monsters, then we need not be troubled by the similarities one might otherwise note between their acts and our own occasional impatience with those whom we most love. In the end, though, we came away from their stories unconvinced that they were different from us in kind. None of the mothers killed because they did not know better or thought that killing a child was acceptable.

Ultimately, it became clear to us that these women's crimes were informed by their circumstances and their backgrounds. In their cruel acts toward their children, these mothers represented the far end of a spectrum among mothers, along which are found many whose acts qualify as abuse or neglect of a less virulent sort. There are those who hit their children. There are those whose cruelty is limited to words, to tone of voice, or simply to what they fail to say or do. We do not yet know why, under similar circumstances, some mothers respond with violence, while others are able to refrain from it. Even if we could not imagine committing their acts ourselves, once we listened to these mother's stories, we could empathize with the emotional turmoil and the helplessness that they felt at the time of their children's deaths.

Once we situated these women on this spectrum, we found it impossible to listen to their stories and maintain our conviction that they were, in some fundamental way, different from us. This is not to say that, as we came to see the impulses underlying their actions as familiar, we necessarily excused them. Nor did we come to feel that, because their acts might be seen as a product of their life experiences, they should be excused. Nonetheless, the stories the women told us served to reshape our sensibilities about guilt, punishment, and prevention.

Policy Implications of Our Study

Although there were many variations in the stories told to us by the incarcerated mothers, when it came to matters of guilt, there were two common threads: first, there was more than one person to blame for the children's deaths, and second, in retrospect, there were at least one or two, and typically more, individuals who could have prevented their deaths. These themes should inform our thinking about how we punish these women, as well as how we go about preventing such crimes in the future.

Punishment

Our criminal justice system embraces a norm of individual accountability and has little use for nuances when it comes to assessing blame. On close examination, however, at least in these cases, there is blood on more than one set of hands. Consider the matter of moral accountability, if not guilt, in any of the eight stories featured in this book. There was the role played by the man who raped and impregnated Laurie, and then left her to contend with the consequences of his acts. There was the drunken indifference of Patty's mother, who tolerated and even enabled her daughter's lover to abuse her. There was Nadine's family—her mother who left her children with their violent father, and her father who moved into and out of her life, raping and beating her. There were the women's fathers, boyfriends, lovers, and husbands, none of whom viewed the care of their children as a moral imperative in their own lives.

In spite of our sense that others share some of the responsibility for the deaths of the children in these cases, we nonetheless believe that it was just and fair to hold the women legally accountable. More difficult is the task of explaining why the women, alone, should be imprisoned, and for how long.

Conventional criminal justice theory holds forth three justifications for punishing one who commits a crime: deterrence, rehabilitation, and retribution. The deterrence rationale for punishing crime is twofold. First, there is the notion that one must punish a given act because it will deter the individual from committing that act again in the future. In order for this explanation to be persuasive, one must imagine a criminal actor who makes a conscious choice to commit her crime, and who might have made a different choice if she knew she would be punished.

Overwhelmingly, the women with whom we spoke were heedless of the law when they killed their children. Those such as Vanessa or Marlene, whose children died as a result of their inaction, did not understand themselves to be risking their children's lives, let alone courting criminal liability, by their failure to properly care for their children. Their fatal mistakes in not obtaining medical treatment for their children resulted from their fear of losing custody. From their perspective, visits to health care providers were not opportunities for helpful interactions. Instead, such visits represented potentially costly endeavors, not only in terms of money, but also in terms of family disruption. They did not intend to harm their children by keeping them from the doctor; in a perverse sense, they were motivated by love. The threat of punishment was there already, in the form of losing custody, and it helped drive them away from care. No amount of threatened punishment seems likely to have changed that outcome.

Nor does the goal of deterrence help to explain why and how we punish the women who deliberately killed their children. Those who acted purposely when they killed their children tended to be either planning a suicide, in which case the threat of punishment held no sway, or they were acting impulsively. The spontaneous acts that led to their children's demise could not have been deterred by a threat of punishment.

The second deterrence-based rationale is the notion of general deterrence. Under this theory, abhorrent acts must be punished so that the public as a whole will refrain from engaging in them. This rationale is particularly forceful in the context of crimes that lack widespread moral condemnation. For instance, laws prohibiting speeding are necessary because we know that without them, people would drive faster and, as a result, we all would be less safe. This rationale is implausible in the context of filicide. It simply defies human experience to posit that it is the threat of punishment, rather than strongly held moral convictions against harming children, that stops more parents from killing their offspring.

The goal of rehabilitation also is a commonly cited justification for incarceration. In recent years, a trend toward punitive sentencing practices, coupled with limited funding for prison inmates, has rendered rehabilitation within prison a hollow promise.[4] Indeed, to the extent that a criminal justice system predicates the need for incarceration on the desire to rehabilitate prisoners for reentry into society, one would expect to see a substantial investment in both prison programming and in the way we evaluate prisoners to determine whether they have been rehabilitated. Instead, the U.S. criminal justice system's funding patterns emphasize a high

priority on mechanisms for restraining prisoners, coupled with a notori-
ously arbitrary parole process.[5]

In spite of this funding preference, prison did seem to have rehabilitated, or at least to have helped these women. Prison stabilized them, providing a structured, predictable environment where they could begin accepting responsibility for their past acts and thinking consciously about
how they wanted to live. Most had availed themselves of the various programs offered within the reformatory. They had completed their educa-
tions, pursued professional training, obtained treatment for addictions and
other health problems, and taken parenting classes. In spite of the limited
nature of the resources in their prison, the overwhelming majority of the
women had taken steps — often significant ones — toward their personal
rehabilitation.

As they spoke to us about their recoveries, giving voice to a newfound
sense of self-love, we tended to feel a strange ambivalence. We were happy
for them, but at the same time, we were still troubled by the enormity of
their crimes. We worried that, in the move to recovery, there might not
have been sufficient accounting made for the babies whose lives they had
taken. Consider Celina, who subjected her daughter to years of physical
abuse and ultimately beat her and left her to die. There was something
chilling to us in her expressed belief that her incarceration was the vehicle
for bringing Jesus into her family's life: "Me being here is [the] reason why
most of my family is being saved today. . . . My soul was dying; I used to see
death. I would see myself in a casket. Little did I know it was my daughter.
She was my lifesaver, saved my soul. I know she lives in my heart." Our
discomfort with Celina's rapid road to salvation speaks to a distinct motive
in punishment. It seemed clear that, although we wanted these incarcerated women to recover, rather than remaining trapped in self-loathing, we
wanted that recovery process to be a slow and thorough one.

In spite of the empathy we felt for many of the women we interviewed,
we found that, in addition to looking to prison for rehabilitation, we also
viewed their incarceration as a punishment. Retribution, an instinctive
and often unspoken human impulse, is the third justification for criminal
punishment. The women's sentences were not based on how long it might
take them to be rehabilitated and ready to return to the outside world. If
that was the only goal, then it was apparent that many of the women with
whom we spoke had long been ready to live outside of the confines of the
reformatory. Indeed, from the stories they told, it seemed likely that they

now stood a better chance of living a clean, loving life, and of making a meaningful contribution to the lives of others, than did most of their families on the outside.

Retribution is an uncomfortably abstract, and even unprincipled goal in the context of these women's cases. After all, to the extent that our need to punish is driven by the harm they caused to their children, as we have seen, there were others who also were blameworthy and yet escaped any punishment. And to the extent that we punish these women because the loss of their children's lives is a loss to us all, it seems clear that most of their children were vulnerable to harm long before they lost their lives. If we view ourselves as collectively harmed by their loss, and therefore collectively invested in their survival, then there was much that we could have done to prevent their deaths.

Perhaps we incarcerate these women in part because they remind us of the flaws we possess, both as individuals and as a whole. They reflect the potential within us all for harm, hate, and despair. They expose the cracks in our system, and their life stories make us uncomfortable. When we hear them with open hearts, we recognize ourselves to be creatures that are not fully autonomous, but rather, the beneficiaries of luck and grace. We are susceptible to random external forces that might just as easily have made our lives infinitely more difficult than they now are.

Many of the women reminded us of this when we interviewed them. One woman said, "You could hit a child when a child runs in front of your car and that's a child-related crime." Another invoked the same metaphor, saying, "You could kill someone on the way home from here in your car and that is vehicular homicide." These women's efforts to normalize their actions, to make us recognize that we might just as easily have been in their places, triggered a reflexive response to distance ourselves from them. We would not hit a child with a car, and if, heaven forbid, we did, we would not be guilty of the same level of crime that these women had committed. We would not be to blame, or at least not entirely to blame. But if one pauses and attempts to imagine the details that might have surrounded the crash, our blamelessness might just as easily dissipate. We might have been distracted, backing up the car without looking in the rearview mirror, or speeding home through a residential area while talking on a cell phone. But we would not have intended to harm the child we hit. And of course, that was precisely their point.

Understood more broadly, the point these women were making was an important one. They did not consider themselves to be blameless, but they nonetheless felt that those who sat in judgment had not seen them, and their actions, in context. Punishment reinforces the myth of personal accountability. One is deemed healthy, or rehabilitated, to the extent that one internalizes that myth, learning to view oneself as blameworthy and accountable. Ultimately, these stories teach us that personal accountability is a partial truth, at best. Therefore, to the extent that we are to honor the memories of the children whose lost lives are at the center of these stories, we must turn to the task of prevention.

Prevention

In retrospect, it is easy to see how things could have been different — how, in each of the women's stories, one person's intervention could have saved the children's lives. As they looked back on their crimes, the women often expressed their belated recognition that they had been living in a toxic situation and that they had been blind to the escape routes that were available to them. One woman with whom we spoke was incarcerated after killing her behaviorally disordered stepchild. She offered this perspective on her actions:

> The children's mother walked away and everyone thought she was so horrible. I then have to think that maybe she was the smarter woman. I think they probably really just need to offer more resources to women. Maybe talk more about the pressures that they deal with. Men all the time take off when a situation is more than they want to deal with and there isn't that stigma attached to them. I think my husband was so happy to have someone else there to take over and give him a break and I was too stubborn to think I could come into a situation that was so broken and fix it.

Because so many of the women had survived abusive interpersonal relationships, and had since received counseling to help them recognize the harm in such relationships, many spoke about domestic violence when asked about how their crimes might have been prevented. Nadine, whose husband killed her son, notes that battered women's options tend to be limited: "Even hillbilly hick towns need resources. Listen. [Don't simply say,] 'I know him and he wouldn't do that.' [There are] two-thirds more animal shelters in Ohio than domestic violence shelters. I was facing seventy-six years and I told God if I didn't have to do that I'd be a spokesperson for women and children. I did not lose one child, I lost all my children."

In most cases, though, it is hard to blame the child's death simply on the fact that the women were involved with violent men. As Vanessa, acknowledged, her child's death was not simply a result of her having tolerated a violent partner:

> I take responsibility for her death because I thought I was doing the right thing but I wasn't. Her passing was an eye opener for me. I was not doing what I was supposed to be doing. Living in an abusive relationship, he was beating me, and sometimes the kids, too. I just kept it secret. . . . My pride played a big part, too. If I thought I didn't like you, [I] wouldn't answer questions. Instead of asking for help, trying to do everything on my own.

Asking for Help

Almost all the women noted that things could have come out differently had they only been willing to ask others for help. In retrospect, the women with whom we spoke were in desperate straits as mothers, although most had grown accustomed to their situations and did not recognize themselves or their children as being at risk. And much of the strife in their daily lives was so commonplace as to be banal. As one of the women from our first set of interviews remarked:

> I want to speak to people about crime period. . . . I would tell them that it can happen to any one of us at any given time. It happened to our family. I'm the one. . . . Just like it happened to me it can happen to you. It could be you. . . . Don't judge anyone for any crime. Everyone gets to the point where they're going to break no matter what. Marriage, school, bills, anything. Everyone has a breaking point and I am tired of people not knowing. It is hard to talk to somebody and ask for help. Maybe people will realize that the mother needs some time off. I'd be glad to take the children or help with your bill. Don't be ashamed. There's nothing to be ashamed about. . . . Don't be judgmental. Try to feel someone else's pain.

Often, the women felt as though, in retrospect, they actually had resources in their lives that they had failed to recognize. For instance, one woman killed her children at a time when she felt overwhelmed. She had decided to commit suicide, and in her desperation, she could not see a way to provide for her children after her death. Looking back on that time in her life, she regrets not having seen her children's occasional babysitter as a resource: "The babysitter thought of me as a friend more than I did of her. I just wanted to make sure she cared for the kids OK. I regret that I didn't see a friend there. She had more practical knowledge on child rearing than I did."

Likewise, Laurie, who committed neonaticide after concealing her pregnancy from her family, noted that the best way to have prevented her crime lay in telling someone and asking for help: "I've been thinking about it all these years. Mom, Dad, my stepdad, my stepmom all say I should've gone to them for help. I want to kick myself because I didn't go to them. I was just thinking about myself."

The Roadblock of Fear

The simple solution of asking for help begs the question of why it is that the women failed to do so. Several factors underlie their reluctance to seek help. First, there is shame inherent in confessing even a minor struggle with motherhood. In our culture, women are expected to cope with, and indeed, to revel in motherhood.[6] Motherhood is considered instinctive, and maternal altruism is a force that society takes for granted.

But the stories told by the vast majority of women we interviewed suggest that it would have been futile to expect help from their families. Time and again, their families had proven themselves to be unreliable and even treacherous. A lifetime of experience had taught them that, although their families might have looked to them for assistance, these women could not expect the same in return. Thus, any true support for these women would have to have come from outside their families. And yet, they were afraid to seek such assistance because they recognized that the admission that they were struggling with the tasks of motherhood might have triggered the state's scrutiny of their children's welfare.

Herein lies the most significant roadblock to preventing filicide: the lack of nonjudgmental resources for mothers and children. One of the women from our first set of interviews explained this fear:

> Most women who abuse their child are hurting inside and need help. Then, the legal system wants to take your children and you have lost. That's the last thing you want is to be separated from your kids, so women won't reach out. We have to get to the root of the problem.

Women need help. They're hurting. Help — if I could ask for help, it would have been prevented. Child care would have helped. Women need an outlet. Children's services could have day care where moms could do drop offs for an hour. Somebody outside of the family.

At the present, the primary goal of state-run child protection agencies is to assess whether a child is at risk of harm. The goal of protection carries with it the understanding that a child who is at risk must be removed from his or her environment. Because the law mandates reporting to the state by those who see children in an official capacity, and who suspect that a child is at risk of harm, struggling mothers may hide their difficulties from those who might be able to help them.

For all the ways in which they varied from one another, the women with whom we spoke were consistent about their passionate desire to keep their children. In their minds, there was little to be gained, and much to be lost, by seeking help from any agency or individual who posed a threat to their household. The punitive posture lends a perverse irony to child protection programs — in the minds of those who most need their help, these agencies represent forces to be avoided, rather than resources. Perhaps the most important step society could take toward preventing at least the unintentional, neglect-related death of children, which constitutes the largest subcategory of maternal filicide, lies in creating nonpunitive respite care and mentoring programs for mothers.

Conclusion

Primary love is observable only in its breach. If satisfied, it brings forth a quiet sense of well-being. . . . If not, it calls forth vehement demands.[7]

The lessons we learned over the hours we spent talking with these women were not confined to the subject of mothers who kill. In retrospect, it seems that their stories taught us broader lessons than we might have expected before embarking on this project.

The first lesson was obvious to us within thirty minutes of beginning our first interview. In important ways, these women were raised in different worlds from the one that we knew. In talking with them, we became aware of the awesome grace and bounty in our lives. Once we understood how many forces had conspired to smooth our roads for us, we could no longer sit easily in judgment of them. Had things been different, we might well have been them.

The second lesson we learned was an awareness of the fact that we are all more than the worst thing that we have done in our lives. Sister Helen Prejean observed as much in her work with death row inmates in Louisiana and elsewhere.[8] The women with whom we spoke had committed one of the darkest acts imaginable. The notion of a mother killing her own child shakes the foundations of our core conceptions of love, trust, and altruism. And yet, these women spoke to us not as monsters, but as people who were capable of kindness, who often were aware of and grateful for the commonplace joys in their lives, and who undertook, day by day, what seems to us, at the end of this project, to be the central task in their lives, as in our own: creating bonds of love and connection with others. As one woman, who had lived for more than a quarter of a century in prison for puposely killing her children, described herself and her evolution:

> It gives me a feeling of achievement when I can help someone else. Not truly that . . . but a fringe benefit. The bad parts of me, I think I have suppressed them so much that I don't need [to hate myself.] . . . I have no grudge and I go on from here. There is no reason to nurture it. . . . So there's nothing exceptionally good, nothing exceptionally bad about me. I'm OK. . . . I hate what I did, I accept that I can't change it — I try to go on — I hope I don't make a mockery with their deaths in the process.

Appendix A

Methodology

The case studies presented in this book are based on two sets of interviews. All interviews took place at the Ohio Reformatory for Women (ORW). The ORW is located in Marysville, Ohio, and is the only prison for women in the state. The first set of interviews were conducted by Cindy Weisbart, Dawn Bramley, Abby Goldstein, Michelle Rone, Kelly White, and Cheryl Meyer, and occurred between April 2001 and December 2001. During that time period there were 69 women in the ORW who were incarcerated for killing their children (out of approximately 1,800 inmates). Forty of these women participated in the study. Of the remaining 29, 13 were unable to be interviewed because they were either in pre-release (9), the residential treatment unit (2), lockup (1), or on judicial release (1). One woman killed her adult son and was not invited to participate. Two women had scheduling difficulties. Only 13 women out of 69 refused to participate.

Of the original 40 interviews, three were discarded from analysis. One was discarded because the victim was her niece. A second interview was discarded because the woman did not answer the questions but rather free associated, providing uninterpretable information. A third interview was later discarded because the women insisted she did not commit the crime and therefore could not answer the questions. Of the 37 women who remained 14 were convicted of murder, 22 of involuntary manslaughter, and 1 of voluntary manslaughter. In one case the woman killed her stepchild, for whom she was the primary caretaker. The average age of the women was 32 at the time of the interview and 24 at the time they committed the offense. They had served an average of 7 years. Fifty-seven percent admitted their guilt. The average age of the children they killed was 5 years old, and 58 percent of the victims were females. The most predominant method used to kill their child was drowning (48%), assault (14%), neglect (14%), smothering/suffocation (14%), and fire (10%). The majority of the cases would have been categorized as abuse-related filicide (30%), followed by assisted/coerced filicide (24%), purposeful (22%), neglect

(16%), and neonaticide (8%). This is in contrast to the data found in our first book, drawn from news stories. There, most cases were purposeful (36%), followed by neglect (35%), neonaticide (17%), abuse (7%), and assisted/coerced (5%).[1] This suggests that the mothers who receive extensive news coverage are not necessarily the same mothers who are incarcerated.

Each woman was called, individually, to the interview site, which was on the campus of the ORW. When they arrived, they were informed that they were being asked to participate in a study on mothers who had been convicted of killing their children. The consent process involved a detailed explanation of the questions we would be asking, of our background and interest in the topic, and of our goals in eliciting information from them. Additionally, the women were also informed, both in writing and verbally, that the interviews could not be shared with the parole board or the Ohio Department of Rehabilitation and Corrections.

If they agreed to participate, each woman was presented with the following eight questions:

1. Tell me about what your life has been like, growing up as a youngster, up until now?
2. What was going on in your life at the time your child died (precipitating events, increased stress)?
3. Did anyone know you were going through a difficult time? Who were the people you confided in and what help did they offer?
4. In your own words, tell me about what happened.
5. How do you think this could have been prevented?
6. How do you feel you have been treated by the system (the police, the courts, etc.)?
7. What changes would you make to the "system" in general?
8. If you had three wishes for the future, what would they be?

The women could answer any or all the questions. Most women chose to answer all the questions in the order they were presented. Each interview lasted approximately two to three hours.

There were two researchers at each interview. One researcher conducted the interview, engaging with the women and asking follow-up questions, while the other researcher acted as a note taker. Prison regulations prohibited video or audio taping. Instead, detailed notes were taken during each interview and were later transcribed. After the notes were transcribed, three of the interviewers independently coded the interviews for details related to the crime, demographics, and background information. If there were discrepancies in coding, the discrepancy was discussed until a consensus was reached.

The following details emerged as consistent topics, mentioned by multiple women and were coded by the interviewers:

Age of mother and child at the time of the incident, charges and sentence, information about accomplices, gender of child, information related to postpartum syndromes, whether the mother admitted guilt, the method of death, how many children were killed, whether drugs or alcohol was involved in the incident, the mother's level of involvement in the death, the mother's relationship with remaining children, whether the women indicated that prison saved them, any discussion of the role of spirituality in their life, opinions related to services in prison, opinions related to the legal system, what the mother currently says about the child she killed, whether children's services had been involved in the case prior to the child's death, whether the mother indicated there had been prior abuse, whether the mother was in a relationship at the time of the child's death and the description of that relationship, whether the mother had been physically or sexually abused as a child, whether the mother had suffered a trauma or loss within a year of the child's death, whether the mother had sought the help of others, whether the mother was homeless in the year prior to the incident, whether the mother was mentally ill in the year prior to the incident or if she had ever been mentally ill, whether the mother had a victim of domestic violence, whether the mother had suicidal ideation or attempts in year prior to killing or ever, whether the mother had an unstable childhood, whether the mother's current relationship with her family was stable, whether the child was wanted and whether the mother bonded with the child. Finally, the wishes they discussed were coded into categories.

After the interviews, we sought to gain further perspective on the women's crimes and to verify the accuracy of the information we obtained from the interviews. Toward that end, we searched various databases to amplify and verify the women's stories. Primary among these was Lexis-Nexis, a legal and news database that provides full text articles and publications from newsmagazines, regional and national newspapers, newsletters, trade magazines and abstracts, and legal appeals. In the vast majority of cases, the information provided to us by the women matched most of the details provided in official and media accounts of the events.

Prior to writing the present book, we decided that the results would be more meaningful if we were able to reinterview some of the women with whom we had originally spoken. As of January 2006, nineteen of the forty original interviewees remained incarcerated. Ten of those women were contacted to participate in follow-up interviews; only one refused. Of the nine that participated, one continued to deny any involvement in or knowledge of the crime with which she was charged. Ultimately, we referred her case to the Innocence Project (a network of lawyers who work toward exonerating wrongfully convicted individuals). In view of her claims of innocence, the content of her interview was omitted from our study. Of the eight women remaining women, two committed the crime with a partner, two of the children died because of abuse, two died from neglect, one died from neonaticide, and one death was purposeful.

The second set of interviews was conducted in January and February 2006 by Thea Jackson, Cheryl Meyer, and Michelle Oberman. As in the original interviews, each woman was called to an interview site, told of the purposes and procedure of the study, reminded of her prior participation, and asked if she wanted to participate in a second interview. The women once again were informed, both in writing and verbally, that the interviews could not be shared with the parole board or the Ohio Department of Rehabilitation and Corrections.

Unlike the first set of interviews, we were able to tailor the questions for each interviewee based on what we knew about the death of her child, both from her prior interview and from the official and media accounts of her case. We drew from the following list of questions for each interview:

I. General

1. One of the patterns we found among mothers who killed their children was that at the time of the crime many of them felt isolated, that they had few supports. Was this a factor for you and/or do you think it is a factor for other mothers?

2. How do you feel about your crime now?

3. Can you describe any involvement that you had with government agencies before your incarceration (e.g., state departments of social services, Child Protective Services, the criminal justice system)?

4. Many of the women we studied who were involved in the killing of their children used drugs and/or alcohol. Was this true for you?

5. Some people say that women who kill their children do it because they want to get revenge against the father of their children. Was this true for you? Do you think it's true in general?

II. Childhood

1. Do you believe childhood experiences have anything to do with mothers killing their children? Explain.

2. Tell us about your childhood. Did you feel loved? Safe? Happy?

3. Tell us about school and work: what did you hope to do when you grew up?

4. What was your educational level when you finished school and were you satisfied with it?

5. Was there violence or abuse in your family growing up?

III. Relationships

1. Tell us about your relationship(s) with the father(s) of your children.

2. Many of the women we studied who were involved in the killing of their children had violent relationships with their partners. Was this true for you?

IV. Mothering

1. How did you cope with the stresses of motherhood?

2. How did/do you view yourself as a mother?

3. Was motherhood different from what you'd expected?

4. What do you think society expects of mothers?

5. Did what you think society expects of mothers affect your behavior in any way?

6. What were your goals as a mother?

7. What were the realities of mothering like for you?

8. How did you support yourself?

V. Mental Illness

1. Often people portray mothers who kill their children as "mad or bad," in other words, mentally ill or evil. How accurate do you think this description is?

VI. Type Specific

A. Assisted/Coerced

1. When we studied mothers who kill their children, we created five different sets of patterns or categories to help us understand. Your case fits the pattern for women who acted with a partner. In many of these cases, the partner usually was not biologically related to the child. Was this true for you? We also found that women who acted with a partner often had abusive relationships with their partner. Was this true for you? In addition, there often was abuse toward the child prior to the fatal abuse. Was this true for you? Do any of these things seem accurate to you regarding mothers who kill their children?

B. Abuse Related

1. When we studied mothers who kill their children, we created five different sets of patterns or categories to help us understand. Your case fits the pattern for women killed their child through abuse. We found that women who killed through abuse had abused the child prior to the fatal abuse, had been involved with state children's services agencies prior to the incident, and came from abusive homes. Do you think any of these things were true for you? Do any of these things seem accurate to you regarding mothers who kill their children?

C. Concealed/Denied Pregnancy

1. When we studied mothers who kill their children, we found that there were five different sets of patterns or categories. Your case fits the pattern for women who concealed their pregnancy. We found that women who concealed their pregnancy often felt guilt, shame, or feared punishment related to the pregnancy. Do you think this was true for you? Do any of these things seem accurate to you regarding mothers who kill their children?

2. Did anyone besides you know that you were pregnant?

3. At the time of your pregnancy, were there any adults in your life whom you could trust?

4. What was the nature of your relationship with the person who got you pregnant?

D. Purposeful

1. When we studied mothers who kill their children, we found that there were five different sets of patterns or categories. Your case fits the pattern for women who purposely killed their children. We found that women who purposely killed their children often felt very close and devoted to their children. Do you think this was true for you? Do any of these things seem accurate to you regarding mothers who kill their children? If so, then the question everyone asks is "Why would they kill their children?" What do you think?

2. We found that women who purposely killed their children also often experienced a significant loss (for example through death or divorce) around the same time as they killed their child. Was this true for you? Do any of these things seem accurate to you regarding mothers who kill their children?

3. When we looked at the women who purposely killed their children, one pattern we found was that they often killed more than one child. When this happened, they killed or attempted to kill all their children. Why do you think they would do this?

E. Neglect

1. When we studied mothers who kill their children, we found that there were five different sets of patterns or categories. Your case fits the pattern for women who killed their children by neglect. We found that these cases involved women whose children were killed by accident rather than on purpose. Was this true for you?

2. Women who killed their children through neglect often were struggling because they did not have anyone who could help them watch their kids. Was this true for you?

3. Women who killed their children through neglect often were facing financial difficulties and had a hard time making ends meet. Was this true for you? Do any of these things seem accurate to you regarding mothers who kill their children?

VII. Incarceration

1. How has your time in prison affected you?
2. Could anything have prevented you from doing this?
3. How do you find meaning in your life now?

Like the original interviews, each interview lasted approximately two to three hours, and there were two researchers at each interview. One researcher primarily conducted the interview, engaging with the women and asking follow-up questions, while the other researcher acted as a note taker. Per Ohio Women's Reformatory regulations, the interviews were not video or audio taped. Instead, detailed notes were taken during each interview, and these notes later were transcribed.

Appendix B

Neonaticide

In view of the frequency of neonaticide among cases of maternal filicide, there were surprisingly few women in our current study who committed this particular crime. Of the original forty women who agreed to speak with us, only three had killed their children in this manner, within twenty-four hours of delivery. Of these, only Laurie remained behind bars when we returned for our second set of interviews. This is not to say that there were not other women in Ohio who were convicted of neonaticide and who served time in the ORW. But, for the most part, these other girls and women received far shorter sentences than did Laurie.

Although Laurie's crime was, in many ways, a typical example of neonaticide, what was unusual about her crime, and what likely earned her a relatively long prison sentence, was the fact that she had been pregnant before, had borne three children, and had previously relinquished a child for adoption. Also, at age twenty-three, she was "old" for this crime. Laurie expressed frustration at the disproportionately long sentence she received, noting that during her incarceration, more than a few women had received significantly shorter sentences for what was essentially the same crime. When they were sentenced to time in the ORW, and not all of them were, their sentences tended to be relatively short; when they appealed these sentences, many were successful in having them reduced. The following subsection explores the neonaticide stories associated with younger mothers.

The (Untold) Neonaticide Story

Throughout history, the crime of neonaticide has been relatively commonplace. The circumstances giving rise to this crime vary across time and culture; a fate associated with disabled newborns in one society might be more common among newborns of unwed mothers in another, and perhaps among female infants in yet another. The thread that runs through all neonaticide stories is the inability of the pregnant woman to set in motion a plan that would permit her either to raise the child she carried, or to safely relinquish it to the care of others.

In contemporary U.S. society, the persistence of neonaticide is, at first blush, puzzling. After all, with the advent of effective methods of contraception, in conjunction with access to legalized abortion, women today arguably have the capacity to exercise greater control over reproduction than at any point in human history. Today's U.S. neonaticide stories demonstrate the way in which the choice to become a mother may be limited by factors that extend well beyond access to contraception and abortion.

In our first book on women who kill their children, our data consisted of filicide cases appearing in the U.S. media in the decade from 1990 to 2000. Of the hundreds of cases mentioned during that time frame, we focused our study on 219 cases that we could follow from start to finish. Of these, thirty-seven cases (17 percent) involved the crime of neonaticide. These cases cast light on this particular story, which was not fully represented by the women we interviewed at ORW.

Isolation and Denial in Neonaticide Cases

Women who commit neonaticide tend to be young; although the ages of women whose neonaticide cases were included in our original book ranged from fifteen to thirty-nine, the average age was nineteen. Not only were the women young, but also, they tended to be single. Indeed, all but one of the women who committed neonaticide was unmarried, and the overwhelming majority of the men who fathered these infants were absent from the women's lives by the time they gave birth.

These women also shared similar emotional realities. One of the most striking features of their stories was the extent to which they were isolated, not only from their sexual partners, but also from trusting relationships with family and friends. To the extent that one might identify a "motive" for the crime of neonaticide, it is fear of disclosure. These young women consistently expressed their fear that they would be exiled from their families, and cut off from their entire support system, should their pregnancies be discovered.

Judging from the outside, in at least some of the cases, the young women's fear of disclosure might seem to be exaggerated. Unwed motherhood is common in contemporary U.S. society, as is premarital sexual activity. As a result, it is difficult to imagine that any parent would respond to her daughter's sexual activity and pregnancy, by evicting her and cutting her off, financially and otherwise.

What is essential to understanding these neonaticide stories is that it is not the reality of the parents' likely response that matters; rather, it is the pregnant girls' fears that animate her actions. The girls who commit neonaticide exhibit standard adolescent behavior — focusing on short-term problems, rather than anticipating long-term consequences of their actions. Their fear of the short-term discomfort of disclosing and confronting their pregnancy leads them to deny it.

Over time, the denial becomes convincing, and the "magical thinking" of adolescence takes hold. They come to believe that they are not pregnant, or that they are not carrying a baby, or that they will miscarry. Dr. Margaret Spinelli, a forensic psychiatrist at Columbia University who has worked with many girls and women who have committed neonaticide, notes that this denial is so profound that, when it comes time to deliver their babies, these women typically describe what amounts to a dissociative episode during childbirth.[1] Their denial takes on dissociative features, and they simply are not mentally present during the labor, delivery, and homicide deaths of their newborns. As such, many later express shock and horror on learning what happened to their infants.

The denial at work in neonaticide cases is not limited to the women who commit the crime. Instead, denial emerges as a learned coping mechanism; one that the adults in their lives seemed to embrace as deeply as did the pregnant girls and women. Consider Laurie who lived with her own parents during her pregnancy and yet, her parents managed to remain unaware of Laurie's condition.

One of the mothers of an Ohio teenager convicted of neonaticide explained that she thought that her daughter was just putting on a little weight, but because she was not dating anyone, she never considered that she might be pregnant. Even today, years after the event, this mother still denies that her daughter actually killed her baby.[2] Another girl repeatedly told her mother she needed health insurance and asked her mother whether she thought she was getting fat. Her mother, touching her belly, told her that she was fine.[3]

The families of the adults in these girls' lives may, in fact, love them, but it is not accurate to assume that the girls, alone, were responsible for "hiding" their pregnancies. The girls did not trust the adults in their lives to respond with compassion to their dilemma, and their lack of trust may well have been a response to the adults' behavior toward them. It is difficult to evaluate the emotional depth of a relationship from the outside, but it certainly bears noting that these adults were sufficiently detached from these young women that they did not notice, or did not want to notice, the signs of pregnancy — emotional and physical. Their detachment and denial underscored the girls' sense of isolation, as well as their faith that their pregnancies would somehow disappear.

One of the more complicated emotional underpinnings of neonaticide seems to be linked to the absence of deep, trusting relationships in these young women's lives. Although they typically were convinced that they could not raise this child, under their present circumstances, they may also have longed for a child, seeing it as a source of love and connection.[4]

The Patterned Nature of Neonaticide as a Form of Homicide

Neonaticide stories become even more patterned when they draw to a close. When they finally go into labor, the overwhelming majority of these young women mistakenly believe that they need to defecate. They spend hours alone, on a toilet, laboring silently. That they are able to endure labor in silence is shocking, given that birth typically is a noisy process. The fact that they are able to pass hours uninterrupted in the bathroom, when, more often than not, family members are in the house with them, underscores the extent to which these girls are emotionally and physically isolated from those who ostensibly should be their support system.

Once their babies are born, most of these young women behave in a manner that demonstrates their exhaustion, panic, and again, their denial. Amazingly, in view of the long months of a pregnancy, those who commit neonaticide seldom are prepared for contending with labor, delivery, and their newborn. Instead, the young women behave impulsively, typically worrying first about being discovered. Rather than pulling the baby out of the toilet, many of them leave the baby to drown while they attempt to clean up the blood and tissue that accompanies childbirth. Others suffocate or strangle their newborns moments after birth, in an effort to silence them.

These women's acts seldom seem premeditated; indeed, the hallmark of neonaticide is the failure to plan ahead. The babies' bodies typically are not concealed; instead, they tend to be found inside, or in the immediate vicinity of, their homes.[5] Sometimes, the women make no effort to hide the bodies, taking them into bed with them or leaving them in the bathroom. Others wrap their babies' bodies and take them back to their rooms, leaving them in the closet, or under the bed. Still others throw the babies' bodies away, not concealing them, but simply placing them in the trash.

In responding to their crimes, just as in responding to their pregnancies, those who commit neonaticide reveal themselves to be experts at denial. They have no plan to cope with labor and delivery, because they are in denial about the fact that they are pregnant. Once their babies are born, they opt to prolong the denial by cleaning the mess and killing the baby, hiding the corpse. Then, when the corpse is found, they often deny that killed it, maintaining instead that it was stillborn or that they do not remember what happened.

Laurie is typical in this regard. Her powerful capacity for denial runs through her life. It enabled her to cope with the violence in her marriage, it permitted her to ignore the rape by her stepfather's best friend, and in the end, it led her to commit neonaticide. To this day, Laurie falls back on denial to cope with her daily life. Indeed, her insistence that prison has been "a lifesaver" for her might be seen as a way of denying even the impact of her incarceration.

Punishing Neonaticide: Laurie's Story and Those Untold

The criminal justice system responds in a wide variety of ways to women who commit neonaticide. Despite the consistently harsh public condemnation that these cases generate, some juries and judges are lenient with these defendants. It is not unusual for those who investigate these cases to elect not to file criminal charges, or for women convicted of neonaticide to receive probation rather than a prison sentence.[6] Indeed, in many countries throughout the world, infanticide laws specify that no charge higher than manslaughter may be brought against these women, and the standard punishment involves probation, coupled with mandatory counseling. This is not to say that neonaticide always is treated leniently; many women who commit this crime are convicted of murder and serve lengthy sentences.[7]

Laurie was troubled by the fact that her sentence was so much longer than that received by others who committed the same crime. In a sense, she is right. During the years in which Laurie was incarcerated, there were at least two high profile-Ohio neonaticide cases that resulted in convictions. These two defendants, Audrey Iacona and Rebecca Hopfer, both served shorter sentences than did Laurie, in spite of the fact that they were charged and convicted of homicide.[8] Audrey Iacona, who was seventeen at the time of her crime, served twenty months of an eight-year sentence, before a judge in 2001 resentenced her to probation and community service. Rebecca Hopfer, also seventeen at the time of her crime, served eight years of a sentence of fifteen to life. In 2004 the Ohio Parole Board granted her clemency.

On the face of it, the difference in punishment appears to be evidence of arbitrariness in the criminal justice system. On closer examination, however, there are several seemingly significant factual differences between the Iacona and Hopfer cases, on the one hand, and Laurie's case, on the other. At the time of her crime, Laurie was an adult, the mother of two children, and had already relinquished a third child for adoption. Iacona and Hopfer both were minors, and neither had carried a pregnancy to term. To the extent that part of what distinguishes neonaticide from other forms of homicide is the mental state of those who commit this crime, it is easy to see why the younger defendants, who have never before experienced childbirth, might seem less blameworthy.

Appendix C

Mothers Who Purposely Kill Their Children

Mothers who purposely kill their children were the largest group (36 percent) in our original set of cases involving maternal filicide.[1] In view of this, one might have expected to find the stories of many such women included in this book. In this appendix, we explore some reasons that might account for their relative absence from these pages.

Only nine of the forty women we interviewed purposely killed their children (21 percent). Of these, only five admitted to having purposely killed their children. When we returned to reinterview the women, three still denied they had purposely killed their children, two had been paroled, one was in the in-patient psychiatric unit, and one declined to participate a second time, indicating that it was just too painful to relive the memories. Thus, of the eight women we reinterviewed, Nancy was the only one whose story was reflective of the patterns common among stories involving mothers who purposely kill their children.

Several factors might account for the discrepancy between the percentages of women who purposely killed their child in our first book and in our interview sample. First, it is possible that the figure of 36 percent, drawn from our earlier work, is not an accurate reflection of the *proportion* of purposeful filicides that occurred during the time frame. As discussed earlier, the data on which our first book, *Mothers Who Kill Their Children*, was based was drawn from media discussion of cases that occurred between 1990 and 2000. It is difficult to evaluate the extent to which the percentage of cases in each category represents actual incidence rates. This is particularly true with regard to cases falling into the "purposeful" category, as stories involving mothers who purposely kill their children tend to be highly sensationalized. As such, it is possible that the figure of 36 percent overestimates the actual proportion of purposeful filicides, in that stories involving a mother who purposely kills her child or children may be more likely to receive media coverage than are other types of cases.

On the other hand, this percentage may be an underestimate, in that mothers who kill their children purposely often attempt suicide at the same time. To the extent that the mother succeeds in killing herself, there is little need for ongoing media attention. There is no trial, no conviction, nothing more to be said. Thus, media coverage in such cases may be minimal, and the case might well have been overlooked in our original analysis.

Another set of explanations for the relative paucity of cases involving mothers who purposely killed has to do with the features of the women who commit this type of filicide. When we initially interviewed women in this category, the "purposeful" mothers quickly emerged as distinct from the other women we have described in this book. They were older, better educated, often killed more than one child, and used different methods of killing their children than other women. Their victims tended to be older. They used weapons, such as knives, or in some cases, they intentionally set fires or poisoned their children. Friends and family often described them as devoted, loving mothers.

In contrast to most of the women's stories in this book, women who purposely killed their children tended to have relatively long-term relationships with the fathers of their children. Most of them suffered the loss of a close relationship in the months prior to losing their child, usually through death or divorce. Some of these women were in the midst of bitter custody disputes when they killed their children. Finally, and perhaps most importantly, in most cases, severe mental illness influenced their actions.

Although we have not focused on the role mental illness plays when mothers kill their children, it clearly was a component in most of the stories we heard throughout this project. Indeed, broadly defined, mental illness is a theme that connects most of these women's lives. From personality disorders, to drug and alcohol dependence, to depression, almost all these women were exposed to, and often engaged in, behaviors that would be categorized as pathological by the *Diagnostic and Statistical Manual of Mental Disorders*.[2] When they spoke of their lives, though, "mental illness" was merely a small part of the stories these women told. Instability was a far more dominant theme, and the signs of mental illness — such as depression — often emerged in response to their unstable environments.

In sharp contrast, mental illness precipitated a crisis in the lives of the mothers who purposely killed their children. Often, it was the precipitating cause of their children's deaths. Although by no means the exclusive illustration of this set of stories, perhaps the clearest example of the role played by mental illness in the stories of mothers who purposely kill their children emerges in cases involving postpartum mental disorders. All five of the women we interviewed who admitted to purposely killing their child had struggled with mental illness at some point in their lives. Three women clearly were suffering from postpartum psychosis at time of their crime, although only two raised it as a defense at trial, and neither was successful. Both were sentenced to fifteen years to life. One woman described how she felt and what she was thinking when she killed her child:

> I began experiencing people following me . . . in grocery stores and cars . . . it progressed and got worse. I felt they were hiding in closets at home and under my bed. It got worse and worse . . . they were hiding in my basement . . . the next morning, I sent my twelve-year-old daughter to school and they came up out of the basement and they were at my stove in my kitchen . . . now, this was in my mind — I know now but not then . . . they were going to kill us with knives and scissors and stab us and I couldn't stand the thought of that. . . . I ended up killing my six-month-old son and I tried to kill myself.

Indeed, twenty years later she still bore the physical scars of her suicide attempt. When she reflected on her crime, she said:

> I love all my children . . . like everyone else . . . it devastated me . . . it could have happened to any woman . . . I was wanting to be a mother — something all women want . . . and to be doing something that you never thought about doing or being [was terrible]. . . . It's not like taking drugs or becoming an alcoholic and getting behind the wheel of a car and knowing the consequences . . . but having a baby which everyone does . . . What kind of mother do people think I am? I have this black stain on me. I don't think there's any mother that wants to take the life of their own child — it's a part of her. I have often felt that to have your child die a natural death — it hurts . . . or if someone accidentally hurts them — that hurts real bad . . . but to know as a mother, you have taken the life of your own child — that's horrendous. You don't think much of yourself . . . even though I know I was sick at the time.

Although postpartum illnesses may be a factor in the cases in which mothers purposely kill their children, the women in this category often suffer from broader psychological disorders, as well. For example, Nancy, who had postpartum depression, was suffering from bipolar disorder long before she became pregnant. She had attempted suicide several times in her life. Suicide, attempted suicide, or suicidal ideation, is common among mothers who purposely kill their children. One woman we interviewed, who killed her children and then attempted to kill herself, said: "Killing them was not out of hate. It was a suicide. I could never envision them without me. I could not accept that someone could raise them better than me."

Other experts have noted the preponderance and severity of mental illness in cases involving women who kill themselves and their children. For example, Moskowitz and others reviewed a series of cases involving filicide-suicide and found that all five of the women whose records they studied were classified as mentally ill.[3] Similarly, Friedman and others[4] found that parents of both sexes who committed filicide-suicide frequently showed evidence of mental disorders. They concluded that traditional risk factors for violence may not be applicable to cases involving filicide-suicide.

Our research provides additional support for the proposition that mental illness often plays a role in cases involving mothers who purposely kill their children. In addition, the consequences of mental illness may explain, in part, the fact that so few of these women's stories are included in this book, and perhaps in the mainstream prison population as well.

Notes

Notes to the Introduction

1. Several authors draw on their experience as health care providers when writing about this topic. For example, clinical psychologist Geoffrey McKee interviewed mothers who killed their children in order to provide forensic evaluations of their cases, as well as to aid him in identifying a risk matrix to be used by other forensic psychologists. See Geoffrey R. McKee, *Why Mothers Kill: A Forensic Psychologist's Casebook* (New York: Oxford University Press, 2006). See also Margaret Spinelli, ed., *Infanticide: Psychosocial and Legal Perspectives on Mothers who Kill* (Arlington, VA: American Psychiatric Press, 2003).

2. Cheryl L. Meyer and Michelle Oberman, *Mothers Who Kill Their Children: Understanding the Acts of Moms from Susan Smith to the "Prom Mom"* (New York: New York University Press, 2001).

3. Nine women were interviewed but one interview was not used because the woman maintained she was innocent and is appealing her case.

4. For a description of postpartum illnesses and their role in legal cases, see Cheryl L. Meyer and Taro Proano, "Postpartum Syndromes and the Legal System," in *It's a Crime: Women and Justice*, 4th ed., ed. R. Muraskin (Englewood Cliffs, NJ: Prentice Hall, 2006), 103.

5. John Godfrey Saxe, "The Blindmen and the Elephant," in *Poetry of America: Selections from One Hundred American Poets from 1776 to 1876*, ed. W. Linton (London: George Bell and Sons, 1887), 150.

6. A copy of the questionnaire, along with a detailed description of our methodology, is included in appendix A.

Notes to Chapter 2

1. Adrienne Rich, *Of Woman Born: Motherhood as an Experience and Institution* (New York: Norton, 1976), 118, 218–19, 246–47; Ann Phoenix, Anne Woollett, and Eva Lloyd, *Motherhood: Meanings, Practices and Ideologies* (London: Sage Publications, 1991), 41, 62; Nancy Chodorow, *The Reproduction of Mothering: Psychoanalysis and the Sociology of Gender* (Berkeley: University of California Press, 1978), 11, 30, 57, 209.

2. Sarah Blaffer Hrdy, *Mother Nature: A History of Mothers, Infants, and Natural Selection* (New York: Pantheon Books, 1999), 69.

3. Rich, *Of Woman*, 246–7.

4. Rich, *Of Woman*, 218–19.

5. Chodorow, *Reproduction*, 57.

6. Approximately 75 percent of the women discussed whether their father was in the home. For more than half of that 75 percent, their father was not in the home.

7. See George W. Holden, Robert Geffner, and Ernest N. Jouriles, eds., *Children Exposed to Marital Violence: Theory Research, and Applied Issues* (Washington, DC: American Psychological Association, 1998); Sandra J. Kaplan, ed., *Family Violence: A Clinical and Legal Guide* (Washington, DC: American Psychiatric Press, 1996), 145; Murray A. Straus, Richard J. Gelles, and Christine Smith, *Physical Violence in American Families: Risk Factors and Adaptations to Violence in 8,145 Families* (New Brunswick, NJ: Transaction Publishers, 1990). In a national survey of more than six thousand American families, 50 percent of the men who frequently assaulted their wives also frequently beat their children.

8. Straus, Gelles, and Smith, *Physical Violence*, id.

9. See Kathleen J. Sternberg, Laila P. Baradaran, Craig B. Abbott, Michael E. Lamb, and Eva Guterman, "Type of Violence, Age, and Gender Differences in the Effects of Family Violence on Children's Behavior Problems: A Mega-Analysis," *Developmental Review* 26 (2006): 89–112.

10. Martha J. Cox and Jeanne Brooks-Gunn, eds., *Conflict and Cohesion in Families: Causes and Consequences* (Mahwah, NJ: Lawrence Erlbaum Associates, 1999), 207–9, 327.

11. Approximately 75 percent of the women discussed the age of their first pregnancy. Eighty-two percent of those women became mothers as adolescents.

12. Lynne Henderson, "Without Narrative: Child Sexual Abuse," *Virginia Journal of Social Policy and Law* 4 (1997): 479.

13. Juliet Schor, *The Overworked American: The Unexpected Decline of Leisure* (New York: Basic Books, 1991).

14. Phoenix, Woolett, and Lloyd, *Motherhood*, 41.

15. Rich, *Of Woman*, 53.

16. See, for example, Rich, *Of Woman*; Kathleen A. Kendall-Tackett, *The Hidden Feelings of Motherhood: A Guide to Coping with Stress, Depression, and Burnout* (Oakland, CA: New Harbinger Publications, 2001), 19–92.

17. See generally Naomi Cahn, "Birthing Relationships," *Wisconsin Women's Law Journal* 17 (2002): 163–98; Elizabeth K. Bowman and Howard A. Palley, "Improving Adolescent Pregnancy Outcomes and Maternal Health: A Case Study of Comprehensive Case Managed Services," *Journal of Health and Social Policy* 18 (2003): 15–42; Elizabeth J. Samuels, "Time to Decide? The Laws Governing

Mothers' Consents to the Adoption of Their Newborn Infants," *Tennessee Law Review* 72 (2005): 509–72.

18. Sarah Blaffer Hrdy, "Mothers and Others," *Natural History*, May 2001, http://citrona.com/articlesbysbh.htm.

19. Sally Placksin, *Mothering the New Mother: Women's Feelings and Needs After Childbirth* (New York: New Market Press, 2000), 48–54, noting that one common denominator across more than two hundred cultures, as of the mid-twentieth century, is the large amount of care and energy given to the new mother-baby unit, particularly by the new mother's female relatives; see also Gregory R. Pierce, Barbara R. Sarason, and Irwin G. Sarason, eds., *Handbook of Social Support and the Family* (New York: Plenum Press, 1996), 386–87.

20. Timmen L. Cermak, *A Primer on Adult Children of Alcoholics*, 2nd ed. (Deerfield Beach, FL: Health Communications, 1989), 34–64; Migs Woodside, "Children of Alcoholics: Helping a Vulnerable Group," *Public Health Report* 103 (November–December 1988): 643–48, noting that because alcoholism is a family secret, children rarely seek help, even as adults.

Notes to Chapter 3

1. Adolescent pregnancy rates declined somewhat in recent years. The teen birth rate dropped 30 percent between 1991 and 2002, down to 43 births per 1,000 females ages 15–19. Nonetheless, three-quarters of teen pregnancies are unplanned, accounting for about one-fourth of all accidental pregnancies. Leslie Baldacci, "A Guide to Your Student," *Chicago Sun Times*, August 26, 2005, 69.

2. Michelle Fine and Pat Macpherson, "Over Dinner: Feminism and Adolescent Female Bodies," in *Power/Gender: Social Relations in Theory and Practice,* ed. Lorraine H. Radtke and Henderikus J. Stam (London: Sage Publications, 1994), 219–46; Deborah L. Tolman, "Doing Desire: Adolescent Girls' Struggles For/ With Sexuality," *Gender and Society* 8 (September 1994): 324–42. Girls describe their fear of being too sexual or "losing control" and being branded a "slut."

3. Studies consistently indicate that approximately half of all high school students experience sexual intercourse. "Abstinence Only Fails to Stop Early Pregnancies, Diseases," *USA Today,* July 30, 2007, 10A.

4. International Planned Parenthood Federation. *Confronting Stigma and Discrimination,* Adolescent Forum No. 44, May 11, 2005. Young people often face stigma and discrimination regarding their sexual and reproductive health, seriously limiting their access to quality services. Many argue that stigma and ignorance among teens are the result of the federal government's federal funding for abstinence-only sex education. A 2004 congressional report concluded that over 80 percent of federal grants go to providing abstinence-only curricula that "contain false, misleading, or distorted information about reproductive health,"

including exaggerations about contraceptive failure rates, the physical and mental health risks of abortion, and the health susceptibilities of the gay population. Hazel Glen Beh and Milton Diamond, "The Failure of Abstinence-only Education: Minors Have a Right to Honest Talk About Sex," *Columbia Journal of Gender and Law* 15 (2006): 12–51, at 12.

5. See Joel R. Grossbard, Christine M. Lee, Clayton Neighbors, Christian S. Hendershot, and Mary E. Larimer, "Alcohol and Risky Sex in Athletes and Nonathletes: What Roles Do Sex Motives Play?" *Journal of Studies on Alcohol and Drugs* 68 (2007): 566–69. See also A. Danielle Iuliano, Ilene S. Speizer, John Santelli, and Carl Kendall, "Reasons for Contraceptive Nonuse at First Sex and Unintended Pregnancy," *American Journal of Health Behavior* 30 (January–February 2006): 92–102.

6. Jennifer Manlove and Elizabeth Terry-Humen, "Contraceptive Use Patterns Within Females' First Sexual Relationships: The Role of Relationships, Partners, and Methods," *Journal of Sex Research* 44 (2007): 3–16. See Michelle Oberman, "Regulating Consensual Sex with Minors: Defining a Role for Statutory Rape," *Buffalo Law Review* 48 (2000): 703–84, describing adolescent vulnerability to coercion in sexually intimate relationships.

7. For a discussion of this, see Laura M. Carpenter, "From Girls into Women: Scripts for Sexuality and Romance in Seventeen Magazine, 1974–1994," *Journal of Sex Research* 35 (1998): 158–68. See also Peggy Giordano, Monica A. Longmore, and Wendy D. Manning, "Gender and the Meanings of Adolescent Romantic Relationships: A Focus on Boys," *American Sociological Review* 71 (April 2006): 260–87.

8. Cheryl Hanna, "Women as Perpetrators of Crime: Sex Before Violence: Girls, Dating Violence, and (Perceived) Sexual Autonomy," *Fordham Urban Law Journal* 33 (2006): 437, 440–42.

9. See Katherine Baker, "Sex, Rape, and Shame," *Boston University Law Review* 79 (1999): 663, 675–84.

10. See Oberman, "Regulating Consensual Sex with Minors," 734–52.

11. We asked the women to describe their relationships with the fathers of their children, and as a result, their stories were exclusively about relationships with men. Many of the women mentioned, in passing, that they currently were involved in loving relationships with women. From their brief descriptions, these homosexual relationships did not appear to replicate the patterns that marked the women's heterosexual relationships in the outside world, but that could be because violence in prison is prohibited and results in the women losing their status and being physically isolated from the rest of the population. Additionally, because the topic of current relationships was beyond the scope of our survey, we did not pursue it.

12. Twenty-three women raised the topic of sexual abuse as children, while

fourteen did not discuss it. Sixteen of the twenty-three (approximately 70 percent) who did discuss it indicated they had been sexually abused as children.

13. Mary Gilfus, "Women's Experiences of Abuse as Risk Factor for Incarceration" (Harrisburg, PA: VAWnet, a project of the National Resource Center on Domestic Violence/Pennsylvania Coalition Against Domestic Violence, 2002), available online at http://new.vawnet.org/category/Main_Doc.php?docid=412. See also C. W. Harlow, "Prison Abuse Reported By Inmates and Probationers," NCJ 172879 (Washington, DC: U.S. Department of Justice, 1999). Government surveys of inmates estimate that 43 to 57 percent of women in state and federal prison have been physically or sexually abused and that 20 to 34 percent reported IPV. Women are three to four times more likely than male prisoners to have an abuse history. More in-depth studies reveal higher abuse rates. See Angela Browne, Brenda Miller, and Eugene Maguin, "Prevalence and Severity of Lifetime Physical and Sexual Victimization Among Incarcerated Women," *International Journal of Law and Psychiatry* 22 (May–August 1999): 301–22. Smaller, more in-depth studies have found that 94 percent of women reported severe physical or sexual abuse, 82 percent were abused a children, and 75 percent reported IPV.

14. Browne, Miller, and Maguin, "Prevalence and Severity."

15. Leo Tolstoy, *Anna Karenina*, trans. Constance Garnett (New York: Random House, 2000), 5.

16. The four main types of IPV are physical violence, sexual violence, threats of physical or sexual violence, and psychological/emotional violence. "Intimate Partner Violence Overview," National Center for Injury Prevention and Control, http://www.cdc.gov/ncipc/factsheets/ipvoverview.htm, citing L. E. Saltzman, J. L. Faslow, P. M. McMahon, and G. A. Shelly, *Intimate Partner Violence Surveillance: Uniform Definitions and Recommended Data Elements,* version 1.0 (Atlanta, GA: Centers for Disease Control and Prevention, National Center for Injury Prevention and Control, 2002).

17. "Intimate Partner Violence Fact Sheet," National Center for Injury Prevention and Control, http://www.cdc.gov/ncipc/factsheets/ipvfacts.htm, citing P. Tjaden and N. Thoeness. *Full Report of the Prevalence, Incidence, Consequences of Violence Against Women: Findings from the National Violence Against Women Survey,* Publication No. NCJ183781 (Washington, DC: U.S. Department of Justice, 2000).

18. See Lenore E. Walker, *The Battered Woman* (New York: Harper and Row, 1979).

19. See Walker, *The Battered Woman*, 44–51, 55–70. For a summary of critiques and expansions of Walker's work, see Kit Kinports, "Deconstructing the 'Image' of the Battered Woman: So Much Activity, So Little Change: A Reply to the Critics of Battered Woman's Self-Defense," *St. Louis University Public Law Review* 23 (2004): 155, 168–177; Evan Stark, "Re-presenting Woman Battering:

From Battered Woman Syndrome to Coercive Control," *Albany Law Review* 58 (1995): 973–1026.

20. Walker, *The Battered Woman*, 55–70.

21. Ibid., 45–54. See generally Lenore E. Walker, *The Battered Woman Syndrome*, 2nd ed. (New York: Springer, 2000).

22. Experts cite to three factors in a woman's decision to stay: "1) practical problems in effecting a separation, 2) the fear of retaliation if they do leave, and 3) the shock reactions of victims to abuse." Angela Browne, *When Battered Women Kill* (New York: Free Press, 1987), 29.

23. Jennifer Ducharme, Catherine Koverola, and Paula Battle, "Intimacy Development: The Influence of Abuse and Gender," *Journal of Interpersonal Violence* 12 (August 1997): 590–99. This study found that non-abused respondents scored significantly higher in intimacy than did abused respondents.

24. Walker, *The Battered Woman*.

25. For many years, federal welfare law prohibited both men and married couples from receiving welfare benefits. Women welfare recipients' benefits could be suspended if they had a male partner in the home. Charles Murray, "Welfare and the Family: The U.S. Experience," *Journal of Labor Economics* 11 (1993): 224, 230.

26. Of the thirty-seven women, eight did not discuss their relationship status. Of the remaining twenty-nine, twelve were not in a relationship. And of the final seventeen, only one indicated there were not problems in the relationship.

Notes to Chapter 4

1. See Nicole L. Letourneau, Miriam J. Stewart, and Alison K. Barnfather, "Adolescent Mothers: Support Needs, Resources, and Support-education Interventions," *Journal of Adolescent Health* 35 (December 2004): 509–25.

2. Sally Placksin, *Mothering the New Mother: Women's Feelings and Needs After Childbirth* (New York: New Market Press, 2000).

3. There is a rich literature on the divergent societal expectations placed on wealthy and poor mothers. See, for example, Martha L. Fineman, "Images of Mothers in Poverty Discourse," *Duke Law Journal* 41 (1991): 274–96, and Martha L. Fineman, *The Neutered Mother, The Sexual Family, and Other Twentieth Century Tragedies* (New York: Routledge, 1995).

4. Murray A. Straus and Julie H. Stewart, "Corporal Punishment by American Parents: National Data on Prevalence, Chronicity, Severity, and Duration in Relation to Child and Family Characteristics," *Clinical Child and Family Psychology Review* 2 (June 1999): 55–70; see also Ellen E. Pinderhughes, Kenneth A. Dodge, John E. Bates, Gregory S. Pettit, and Arnaldo Zelli, "Discipline Responses: Influence of Parents' Socioeconomic Status, Ethnicity, Beliefs About Parenting, Stress, and Cognitive Emotional Processes," *Journal of Family Psychology* 14

(September 2000): 380–400; Andrew Grogan-Kaylor and Melanie D. Otis, "The Predictors of Parental Use of Corporal Punishment," *Family Relations* 56 (January 2007): 80–91.

5. See Martha J. Cox and Jeanne Brooks-Gunn, eds., *Conflict and Cohesion in Families: Causes and Consequences* (Mahwah, NJ: Lawrence Erlbaum Associates, 1999), 207–9, 327.

6. See generally Galia Shamir-Essakow, Judy A. Ungerer, and Ronald M. Rapee, "Attachment, Behavioral Inhibition, and Anxiety in Preschool Children," *Journal of Abnormal Child Psychology* 33 (April 2005): 131–43; Kathleen Mc-Cartney, Margaret Tresch Owen, Cathryn L. Booth, Alison Clarke-Stewart, and Deborah Lowe Vandell, "Testing a Maternal Attachment Model of Behavior Problems in Early Childhood," *Journal of Child Psychology and Psychiatry* 45 (May 2004): 765–78.

7. See Barbara B. Woodhouse, "'Who Owns the Child?': Meyer and Pierce and the Child as Property," *William and Mary Law Review* 33 (1992): 995–1122; Odeana R. Neal, "Myths and Moms: Images of Women and Termination of Parental Rights," *Kansas Journal of Law and Public Policy* 5 (1995): 61–71.

8. Neal, "Myths and Moms," 62.

Notes to Chapter 5

1. Women who are serving life sentences without parole go through similar stages. For a discussion, see Sherri Roscher, "Development of Coping Strategies in Female Inmates with Life Sentences," Psy.D. diss., School of Professional Psychology, Wright State University, Dayton, Ohio, 2006.

2. Reginald A. Wilkenson, "Mental Health Care for Ohio State Prisoners: The View from the Director's Office," *Correctional Mental Health Report* (January–February 2000), http://www.drc.state.oh.us/web/articles/article58.htm.

3. *Dunn v. Voinovich*, C1-93-0166 (S.D. Ohio, July 10, 1995).

4. See *Dunn v. Voinovich*. See also Fred Cohen and Sharon Aungst, "Prison Mental Health Care: Dispute Resolution and Monitoring in Ohio," *Criminal Law Bulletin* 33 (July–August 1997): 299–327. Finally, see PBS *Frontline* documentary on mental health care in Ohio prisons, http://www.pbs.org/wgbh/pages/frontline/shows/asylums.

5. The budget for mental health services in 2001 represented 5.1 percent of the ODRC operating budget. In 2006, mental health was allocated 4.21 percent. See Department of Rehabilitation and Corrections Annual Reports, http://www.drc.state.oh.us/web/Reports/reports.htm.

6. Personal communication, Dr. Karen Dapper, Clinical Director of Mental Health Services, Ohio Reformatory for Women.

7. Associated Press, "Enron Founder Ken Lay Dies of Heart Disease," MSNBC Web site, July 5, 2006, http://www.msnbc.msn.com/id/13715925. Fol-

lowing his conviction, Lay told reporters: "I am a lucky man. I am blessed. God is in control. All things will work out for those who believe in God." Amelia H. C. Ylagan, "Obituary of a Corporate Man," *BusinessWorld,* July 17, 2006, S1.

8. Abraham Maslow, "A Theory of Human Motivation," *Psychological Review* 50 (July 1943): 370–96.

Notes to Chapter 6

1. Austin Sarat, " '. . . The Law Is All Over': Power, Resistance, and the Legal Consciousness of the Welfare Poor,' *Yale Journal of Law and Humanities* 2 (1990): 343–79, 344.

2. Eleven women did not discuss childhood physical or sexual abuse. Of the remaining twenty-six, nineteen indicated they had been physically or sexually abused.

3. See Cheryl L. Meyer and Michelle Oberman, *Mothers Who Kill Their Children: Understanding the Acts of Moms from Susan Smith to the "Prom Mom"* (New York: New York University Press, 2001).

4. See, for example, K.H. v. Morgan, 914 F.2d 846 (7th Cir. 1990). A girl was placed in nine foster homes over the course of three and half years and often victimized by beatings and sexual assault. See also Children's Rights Organization, "Child Abuse and Neglect, Read a Child's Story," http://www.childrensrights. org/site/PageServer?pagename=jacksonbrothers. In 2003, the public learned to its horror that New Jersey's Department of Youth and Family Services had visited the Jackson home thirty-eight times during a four-year period but took no action on reports that the children were undernourished; by the time the boys were removed from their home, their teeth had decayed, their stomachs were distended, and not one of the boys weighed more than forty-five pounds).

5. See Kristine Schuerger, "Information Packet: Siblings in Foster Care," *National Resource Center for Foster Care and Permanency Planning,* July 2002, http://www.hunter.cuny.edu/socwork/nrcfcpp/downloads/information_packets/siblings-pkt.pdf, notes studies indicating that state agencies succeed in keeping siblings together less than 25 percent of the time.

6. See Rebecca Winters, "A Miami Child's Disappearance from Foster Care Reveals Cracks in a State's Overburdened System," *Time,* May 13, 2002, 55. See also Shana Gruskin, "Two States Lead the Way to Reform: Illinois, Alabama Find Ways to End Crises in Child Care Similar to Florida's," *Sun-Sentinel,* June 3, 2002, 1A. Illinois suffered through gruesome child deaths, class-action suits, and court-ordered decrees in the early 1990s; it has recovered by reducing caseloads from a caseworker average of forty children per worker to fifteen.

7. Some states, such as California, determine maximum capacity of foster children at the time of licensing based on factors like number of other household members, features of the facility, and ability to comply with state regulations. See

Cal. Code Regs. tit. 22 § 80028 (2006). Florida, for example, offers a flexible guideline that the maximum capacity of the home must be limited and should not exceed five in most cases. Fla. Admin. Code Ann. r. 65C-13.011 (2006).

8. See Laurie M. MacKinnon, *Trust and Betrayal in the Treatment of Child Abuse* (New York: Guilford Press, 1998), 34–36, 60.

9. Approximately 75 percent of the women discussed whether they completed high school. More than half of that 75 percent did not complete high school.

10. See Sara Rosenbaum, Anne Markus, and Colleen Sonosky, "Public Health Insurance Design for Children: The Evolution from Medicaid to SCHIP," *Journal of Health and Biomedical Law* 1 (2004): 1, 7–8. Despite Medicaid's embroiled reputation, it is the nation's single largest source of health insurance. In 2002 Medicaid covered 51 million persons at a cost of over $200 billion.

11. Kaiser Family Foundation, "The Uninsured and their Access to Health Care," October 2006, http://www.kff.org/uninsured/1420.cfm.

12. See Michelle Oberman, "Mothers Who Kill: Coming to Terms with Modern American Infanticide," *DePaul Journal of Health Care Law* 8 (2004): 3, 29; see also Marsha Ginsburg, "Little Lost Souls: Girls Who Throw Away Their Babies — Will Legal Abandonment Law Help?" *San Francisco Examiner*, January 16, 2000, A1, tells stories of multiple young girls who hide their pregnancies due to fear, shame, panic, or lack of knowledge.

13. A discussion of the mechanisms of health care reimbursement is beyond the scope of this inquiry, but it bears noting that our system of compensation for health care providers is diagnosis driven. Doctors get paid according to the diagnoses they make. The more diffuse health care problems that stem from poverty typically do not lend themselves to a succinct diagnosis.

14. Alvin L. Schorr, *Welfare Reform: Failure and Remedies* (Westport, CT: Praeger, 2001), 11–13, 24, describing the gradual process by which Aid to Families with Dependent Children (AFDC) became available to unmarried mothers.

15. See Gwendolyn Mink, "The Day, Berry, and Howard Visiting Scholar: Welfare Reform in Historical Perspective," *Connecticut Law Review* 26 (1994): 879, describing the manner in which a "welfare mother" is stigmatized for having children outside marriage, for not working, for not "choosing" to depend on men; Charles Noble, *Welfare as We Knew It: A Political History of the American Welfare State* (New York: Oxford University Press, 1997), 127, observing that social conservatives felt that the availability of AFDC encouraged single women to have children and caused families to break up.

16. See George Hesselberg, "Reagan's Lies Will Live On, Too," *Wisconsin State Journal*, June 8, 2004, B1.

17. See Catherine R. Albiston and Laura Beth Nielsen, "Welfare Queens and Other Fairy Tales: Welfare Reform and Unconstitutional Reproductive Controls," *Howard Law Journal* 38 (1995): 473, 479–80.

18. Kathleen Kost and Frank W. Munger, "Fooling All of the People Some of the Time: 1990s Welfare Reform and the Exploitation of American Values," *Virginia Journal of Social Policy and Law* 4 (1996): 3, 14.

19. See Charles Murray, "Welfare and the Family: The U.S. Experience," *Journal of Labor Economics* 11 (1993): 224, 230.

20. Jason DeParle, *American Dream: Three Women, Ten Kids, and a Nation's Drive to End Welfare* (New York: Viking, 2004).

21. Austin Sarat, "The Law Is All Over: Power, Resistance, and the Legal Consequences of the Welfare Poor," *Yale Journal of Law and Humanities* 2 (1990): 343, 344.

22. Ibid., 346.

23. See *Santosky v. Kramer*, 455 U.S. 745, 760 (1982). It is impermissible to presume that child and parent have adverse interests prior to a legal finding that a parent is unfit. The child welfare system thus contains an inherent, rebuttable presumption favoring reunification.

24. Steven G. Anderson, "Welfare Recipient Views About Caseworker Performance: Lessons for Developing TANF Case Management Practices," *Families in Society* 82 (March–April 2001): 165–75.

25. MacKinnon, *Trust and Betrayal*, 34–36, discussing factors that shape clients experiences with Child Protective Services caseworkers and noting that some parents view the state's involvement in their lives as mutually chosen — there are self-referrals and consenting referrals.

26. Ibid.

27. John E. B. Myers, ed., *The Backlash: Child Protection Under Fire* (Thousand Oaks, CA: Sage Publications, 1994), 56–57.

28. Many of the women used this term to refer to their court-appointed lawyers.

29. Rape trauma syndrome was first recognized by Ann Burgess and Lynda Holmstrom, *Rape: Victims of Crisis* (Bowie, MD: R. J. Brady, 1974); Burgess and Holmstrom, "Rape Trauma Syndrome," *American Journal of Psychiatry* 131 (1974): 981, 982; Carol C. Nadelson, Malkah T. Notman, Hannah Zackson, and Janet Gornick, "A Follow-Up Study of Rape Victims," *American Journal of Psychiatry* 139 (1982): 1266, 1267; Libby O. Ruch, Susan Myers Chandler, and Richard A. Harter, "Life Change and Rape Impact," *Journal of Health and Social Behavior* 21 (1980): 248–49. Although some researchers have written about the psychological reaction to rape in terms of three or four technical stages of recovery, all agree that the basic stages are an acute stage and a long-term resolution stage.

30. One woman had submitted her case to an Ohio law school to be reviewed by the Innocence Project.

31. See Phillip J. Resnick, "Murder of the Newborn: A Psychiatric Review of Neonaticide," *American Journal Psychiatry* 126 (1970): 1414–15; see also Velma

Dobson and Bruce Sales, "The Science of Infanticide and Mental Illness," *Psychology, Public Policy and Law* 6 (2000): 1098, 1105.

32. Amy Wills, "Comment: Neonaticide: The Necessity of Syndrome Evidence When Safe Haven Legislation Falls Short," *Temple Law Review* 77 (2004): 1001nn 183–86, and accompanying text, documenting the inconsistent treatment of this crime by U.S. courts.

33. See appendix B, discussing these Ohio cases, and general patterns in the crime of neonaticide.

Notes to Chapter 7

1. Mary Jane Weiss, "Hardiness and Social Support as Predictors of Stress in Mothers of Typical Children, Children with Autism, and Children with Mental Retardation," *Autism* 6 (March 2002): 115–30.

2. Trudi Venters Horton and Jan L. Wallander, "Hope and Social Support as Resilience Factors Against Psychological Distress of Mothers Who Care for Children with Chronic Physical Conditions," *Rehabilitation Psychology* 46 (November 2001): 382–99.

3. Cynthia J. Schellenbach, Kathleen Strader, Francesca Pernice-Duca, and Marianne Key-Carniak, "Building Strength and Resilience Among At-Risk Mothers and Their Children: A Community-based Prevention Partnership," in *Resilience in Children, Families and Communities: Linking Context to Practice and Policy,* ed. Ray DeV. Peters, Bonnie Leadbeater, and Robert J. McMahon (New York: Kluwer Academic/Plenum Publishers, 2005), 101–16.

4. See Craig Haney, "Psychology and the Limits to Prison Pain: Confronting the Coming Crisis in Eighth Amendment Law," *Psychology, Public Policy, and the Law* 3 (1997): 499, 523–25, 542–48, explaining the origins of the "just deserts" theory of incarceration, where retribution by the government trumps notions of rehabilitation.

5. Joan Petersilia, "Parole and Prisoner Reentry in the United States," *Crime and Justice* 26 (1999): 479: "Parole, a system that developed in the United States more by accident than by design, now threatens to become the tail that wags the corrections dog" (484).

6. Indeed, there is a cottage industry of books, popular and scholarly, devoted to dismantling the mythology around motherhood as blissful and easy. See, for example, Trisha Ashworth, *I Was a Really Good Mom Before I Had Kids: Reinventing Modern Motherhood* (San Francisco: Chronicle Books, 2007); Andrea J. Buchanan, *Mother Shock: Loving Every (Other) Minute of It* (New York: Seal Press, 2003); Susan Maushart, *The Mask of Motherhood: How Becoming a Mother Changes Everything and Why We Pretend It Doesn't* (New York: New Press, 1999).

7. Nancy Chodorow, *The Reproduction of Motherhood: Psychoanalysis and the Sociology of Gender* (Berkeley: University of California, 1978), 64.

8. Helen Prejean, *The Death of Innocents: An Eyewitness Account of Wrongful Executions* (New York: Vintage, 2006).

Notes to Appendix A

1. Cheryl L. Meyer and Michelle Oberman, *Mothers Who Kill Their Children: Understanding the Acts of Moms from Susan Smith to the "Prom Mom"* (New York: New York University Press, 2001).

Notes to Appendix B

1. See Margaret G. Spinelli, ed., *Infanticide Psychosocial and Legal Perspectives on Mothers who Kill* (Arlington, VA: American Psychiatric Press, 2003).
2. Radio interview with Rebecca Hopfer's parents on *Sounds Local*, WYSO, Yellow Springs, Ohio, January 11, 2002.
3. Michelle Oberman, "Mothers Who Kill," retelling the story of one young woman convicted of neonaticide.
4. Ibid., 63–68.
5. Meyer and Oberman, *Mothers Who Kill.*
6. Michelle Oberman, "Understanding Infanticide in Context: Mothers Who Kill, 1870–1930 and Today," *Journal of Criminal Law and Criminology* 92 (2002): 707, 711.
7. Amy Wills, "Neonaticide: The Necessity of Syndrome Evidence When Safe Haven Legislation Falls Short," *Temple Law Review* 77 (2004): 1001nn183–86, and accompanying text, 1021, documenting the inconsistent treatment of this crime by U.S. courts.
8. Rob Modic, "Hopfer Sentence Commuted: February Hearing Likely for Mom Who Killed Newborn," *Dayton Daily News*, January 16, 2004, A1; Stephen Hudak, "Home Arrest Ends: She Just Wants to Blend In," *Cleveland Plain Dealer*, March 21, 2002, B5.

Notes to Appendix C

1. Cheryl L. Meyer and Michelle Oberman, *Mothers Who Kill Their Children: Understanding the Acts of Moms from Susan Smith to the "Prom Mom"* (New York: New York University Press, 2001).
2. American Psychiatric Association, *Diagnostic and Statistical Manual of Mental Disorders*, 4th ed. (Washington, DC: American Psychiatric Association, 2000).
3. Andrew Moskowitz, A. I. F. Simpson, Brian McKenna, Jeremy Skipworth, and Justin Barry-Walsh, "The Role of Mental Illness in Homicide-Suicide in New

Zealand," *Journal of Forensic Psychiatry and Psychology* 17 (September 2006): 417–30.

4. Susan Hatters Friedman, Debra R. Hrouda, Carol E. Holden, Stephen G. Noffsinger, and Phillip J. Resnick, "Filicide-Suicide: Common Factors in Parents Who Kill Their Children and Themselves," *Journal of the American Academy of Psychiatry and the Law* 33 (2005): 496–504.

Index

About the Authors

MICHELLE OBERMAN and CHERYL L. MEYER are coauthors of *Mothers Who Kill Their Children: Understanding the Acts of Moms from Susan Smith to the "Prom Mom"* (also available from NYU Press). MICHELLE OBERMAN is Professor of Law at Santa Clara University School of Law in Santa Clara, California. CHERYL L. MEYER is Professor of Psychology at Wright State University School of Professional Psychology in Dayton, Ohio. She is also the author of *The Wandering Uterus* (NYU Press).